What Every Woman
Needs to Know
about Abortion

What Every Woman Needs to Know about Abortion

HELENE S. ARNSTEIN

Charles Scribner's Sons · New York

Copyright © 1973 Helene S. Arnstein

Library of Congress Cataloging in Publication Data

Arnstein, Helene S
  What every woman needs to know about abortion.

    1. Abortion—United States.   I. Title.
HQ767.5.U5A75   301   73–5168
ISBN 0–684–13547–7
ISBN 0–684–13559–0 (pbk.)

This book published simultaneously in the
United States of America and in Canada—
Copyright under the Berne Convention

All rights reserved. No part of this book may be reproduced
in any form without the permission of
Charles Scribner's Sons.

1 3 5 7 9 11 13 15 17 19 C|C 20 18 16 14 12 10 8 6 4 2
1 3 5 7 9 11 13 15 17 19 C|P 20 18 16 14 12 10 8 6 4 2

Printed in the United States of America

H G767.5
.U5A76
1973
GTS

Contents

5

CONTENTS

Foreword

The purpose of this book is to guide a woman safely from the time she first believes that she is pregnant—at a point in her life when she has grave doubts about bearing the child—through her decision-making, the abortion itself, and her postabortion care and reactions. In addition to giving factual information, I have tried to emphasize the personal feelings of the individual woman and her emotional reactions at every stage of the experience. Naturally, absolute answers cannot be given to all questions or for all women, but questions and possible solutions are presented in such a way as to help a woman find the answers that are right for her. The term "woman" is generally, though not always, used in the book, since any female of child-bearing age

7

is technically a woman and the repetition of "girl or woman" would become very monotonous.

In order to avoid delay in finding the safest and best facilities for an abortion and in finding counseling help if it is needed in reaching a decision, I strongly recommend that a woman who is considering an abortion get in touch with either of two noncommercial agencies: the Planned Parenthood Federation of America or the National Clergy Consultation Service on Abortion. Both provide consultation and referral services free of charge.

The Planned Parenthood Federation has affiliates in forty-two states and the District of Columbia and is constantly opening new branches. Several of its affiliates are now offering early-abortion services. Check your local telephone directory or that of the nearest large city to find whether there is an affiliate near your home. Should there not be, telephone at once to the national headquarters (address and telephone number in the following list) and ask to be referred to the nearest affiliate.

The National Clergy Consultation Service on Abortion is a group of more than two thousand concerned members of the clergy—ministers and rabbis in many states, who know the ropes and can shepherd you safely through an abortion. When you call the national office (see following list), you will hear a recording giving the telephone numbers of all branches in the United States. Then call the nearest one and you will be given assistance.

Many colleges, universities, and voluntary groups and agencies also provide information and referral service. A woman who knows, or is reliably recommended to, a medical authority or a person in one of the helping professions may wish to turn to that individual for guidance. *Do not contact a commercial abortion-referral agency.*

The following list provides the names and addresses of the national headquarters of organizations mentioned in the text and an indication of the areas in which they can be helpful; local offices of some can be found in the telephone directory of your own town or a nearby city.

The American Psychiatric Association, 1700 Eighteenth Street, N.W., Washington, D.C. 20009. (202) 232-7878.
Will help in locating a qualified psychiatrist in or near your community.
Association for Voluntary Sterilization, Inc., 17 West 40th Street, New York, N.Y. 10018. (212) 524-2344.
Will supply information about sterilization.
The Child Welfare League of America, 67 Irving Place, New York, N.Y. 10003. (212) 254-7410.

Will supply information and help in regard to adoption services, maternity homes, foster-family care, day care centers, family day care services, and services for families and individuals under stress.

The Family Service Association of America, 44 East 23rd Street, New York, N.Y. 10010. (212) 674-6100. Will help in locating a professional social-work counselor near you. A Family Service agency may be listed in your local telephone directory; be sure to ask whether it is affiliated with the national organization. If there is no local affiliated agency, get in touch with the national headquarters.

The National Association for Mental Health, 1800 North Kent Street, Roslyn, Arlington, Virginia 22209. (703) 528-6405. Will give information and help toward locating qualified professionals counseling on family problems. Look in the telephone directory under Mental Health Association to find a local chapter of the Association, or write to the national office.

The National Clergy Consultation Service on Abortion, 55 Washington Square South, New York, N.Y. 10012. (212) 477-0034. Will supply counseling and help on any problem related to unwanted pregnancy; see previous discussion.

Planned Parenthood Federation of America, Inc., 810
Seventh Avenue, New York, N.Y. 10019. (212) 541-
7800.

Telephone or write for the name of the affiliate nearest you (see previous discussion). The national office
will send booklets on contraceptive methods on request, and local branches also give advice on contraception.

1

Abortion, the Woman, and the Law

||||||||||||||||||||||||||||||||||||||||||||||||||||||||||||||||||||||||||

With the United States Supreme Court's sweeping overthrow of state abortion statutes, the law has finally caught up with public sentiment and practice. The revolution in both public and medical attitudes that led to this decision was one of the swiftest social changes ever to take place in United States history.

About a million illegal abortions a year were performed in the United States before states began to reform or repeal their stringent abortion laws. In 1965, only 8,000 legal abortions were performed, but by 1971, according to the Department of Health, Education, and Welfare, the figures had risen to over 480,000. It is now estimated that 1.6 million American women a year will be terminating their pregnancies.

Prior to the early 1960s "abortion" was a whispered word, just as mental illness and cancer were shrouded in secrecy a generation earlier. Few people dared to discuss abortion in public. To many, the word implied disgrace, shame, and sexual promiscuity. It was illegal and criminal. It was "murder." A censorious public was as ready to brand a woman with a red "A" for abortion as were Hester Prynne's contemporaries in *The Scarlet Letter* to brand her for adultery.

Abortion has been known to the human race from time immemorial. Records show that it was practiced in Egypt in 1900 B.C., and most likely primitive abortion methods existed even before then. (Until recently, on one small Caribbean island, a woman wishing to end her pregnancy would have a back tooth yanked out, as the pain and shock were believed to cause a miscarriage. A man would look into the mouth of a prospective wife to see how many abortions she had had.)

Despite the long history of abortion, the illegality has resulted in an amazing lack of valid information about it. This is particularly true concerning the psychological and emotional effects.

The Individual Woman's Response

A woman may experience some unexpected emotional reactions before and after her pregnancy is ended. The

14

main and obvious reason is that the woman seeking an abortion is a *human being* as well as a body. Abortion cannot be taken lightly or compared with a visit to the dentist. An abortion means probing the innermost part of a woman's body, the very core of her femininity. It is a human experience involving a woman's feelings about herself, about the man who got her pregnant, and about her family.

Response to the abortion procedure depends upon many conditions: the woman's age; whether or not this was her first pregnancy; the stage of pregnancy at the time of the abortion (an abortion in a late stage of pregnancy involves more complicated operative techniques as well as more complex emotions); the circumstances under which the woman became pregnant; her use or non-use of a contraceptive (did she fail to use a contraceptive or did her contraceptive fail her?); her state of mental health; her personality—whether she is a person who can take things in stride and cope with crises, or is overly sensitive, easily upset, and prone to severe tensions and anxieties.

Much too depends upon her educational and religious background. If she has been taught that life begins at the moment of conception, she may feel she has destroyed life. If she believes that life begins only when an unborn baby is "viable," that is, able to live outside of its mother's body, she may not feel so troubled. Philosophical, medical, and religious debate over when life begins has been going on for centuries. Life is certainly present in the fertilized egg and even in the unfertilized egg, but no one as yet has been able to determine at what point an embryo or fetus should be regarded as a human being or a member of society. Dr. Robert E. Hall, Associate Professor of Obstetrics and Gynecology at Columbia University College of Physicians and Surgeons, writes: "One can admire St. Augustine for conceding that no one will ever know when fetal life begins" ("Time Limitation in Induced Abortion," 1972).

The woman's attitude toward her abortion is strongly influenced by those of the man involved (will he reject her?), the family (will they chastise her?), and the staff of the hospital or clinic (will they show a sympathetic or a punitive attitude?). Yet there are a variety of individual responses, too:

- Linda, aged seventeen, unmarried, came out of the clinic just a little shaky after her abortion. "It really wasn't as bad as I expected," she told a friend who was waiting for her. Several days later, Linda began to have crying spells. She could not understand why.

- Joan, the thirty-five-year-old mother of a teenaged girl, let her husband persuade her to terminate her pregnancy. Afterward, not at all sure she had made the right decision, Joan resented him for many weeks.

- Elizabeth, young and unmarried, shrugged her shoulders: "It's over. I want to forget the whole thing as soon as possible and I don't want to talk about it."

- Vera, aged twenty-three, quietly revealed her emotions: "As I left the hospital, I felt that everyone on the street *knew* that I had gone for an abortion."

- Barbara, a mother of two school-aged children, smiled happily: "I knew I had done the right thing for all of us and I have no unpleasant afterthoughts."

- Dorothy, an attractive divorcée, executive in a large department store, pointed out how lucky and relieved she was to have been able to get an abortion with so little fuss and with so little discomfort.

To a large extent the emotional response patterns of today's woman seeking abortion are also determined by the influences that have brought about the legalization of abortion after so many years.

Changes in Laws and Attitudes

Before 1967, a woman could get a legal abortion in the United States only if her life was at stake. Despite this restriction, a woman desperate enough and determined enough usually found some means by which to end her problem pregnancy. If she could afford it, she might take a trip to a foreign country where an abortion could be obtained easily. Or she would pay a private physician a tidy sum to abort her. If she had "influence," she could arrange to be admitted to a hospital for a curettage due to "female troubles." If she did not have much money, her problem was more difficult. She could go to a back-alley abortionist or midwife, who did the job under harrowing and unsanitary conditions. Or she would attempt to abort herself. In any case she frequently landed in a hospital having her incomplete or bungled abortion patched up—if it could be patched up. Perforation of the uterus and infection with risk to her life and future ability to have children were common results. Bungled abortions were at one time the most prevalent emergency cases in hospital departments of obstetrics and gynecology. The public health picture was grim.

By the time the Supreme Court handed down its decision on abortion, four states—Alaska, Hawaii, New

York, and Washington—had changed their laws so that a woman could get an abortion "on request"—that is, for any reason. Yet even in these states—except for New York, to which women flocked by the thousands to have their abortions—there were still some ifs and buts. There were residency requirements of thirty to ninety days; there were various rulings on the length of pregnancy (up to the seventeenth week only, in one state); and in one state parental consent was needed for unmarried unemancipated minors.

About fifteen other states had made some reforms enabling a woman to end her pregnancy legally under certain conditions—sometimes interpreted broadly and sometimes literally—yet a number of these states also had residency requirements. The remaining twenty-one states were referred to as "old law" states since they followed statutes dating back to the middle of the nineteenth century.

A woman's fate was determined by where she happened to live; in a "reform" or "old law" state she would be punished and denied a legal abortion (except under various specified conditions) whereas in an "on request" state she could have her pregnancy terminated when she so wished (more or less).

There were other inequities. Certain states would grant a woman permission to end her pregnancy if it could be proven she was psychically unfit to bear a child (mental health clause). Because of this, a woman first had to make an application to a hospital abortion or review board, through a psychiatrist. She needed to find ways of proving herself to be mentally and emotionally unstable—actually demeaning herself thereby as she begged for an abortion. Sometimes, to "convince" her consulting psychiatrist, she threatened suicide. Her psychiatric consultation could well cost up to $150. One girl let herself be committed to a psychiatric division of a hospital at great expense to her before gaining permission for an abortion. As one woman put it, "I see no reason why I have to be judged as severely neurotic and disturbed just because my diaphragm slipped!"

All of this meant, again, that the woman without money was out of luck.

Then there was the period of waiting, sometimes as long as three weeks—often making the difference between a woman's having an early, easy, and safe abortion or a later, more complicated one—while the hospital committee sat in judgment.

The consulting psychiatrist was in a difficult position, as was the gynecologist, whose medical judgment had to be questioned by the state. The psychiatrist had to worry about perjuring himself by pronouncing the woman mentally unstable when he knew in most cases that this was not so. Frequently he had to rely on his own knowledge, wisdom, and judgment, realizing that any woman forced to go through with an unwanted pregnancy often was truly jeopardizing her own and her unborn baby's well-being. In deciding what exactly was a grave threat to a woman's physical or mental health, many doctors went along with the World Health Organization's definition of health as "a state of complete physical, mental and social well-being, not only the absence of illness and disease."

The Supreme Court's ruling on abortion was the culmination of a change in medical, philosophical, sociological, psychological, religious, and moral attitudes that had been taking place for some time. Specifically, this shift in attitudes and practice can be attributed to social forces which dramatically swayed public opinion by bringing into focus the absurdities, hypocrisies, cruelties, and dangers of most abortion laws.

Sexual mores. There had been a rapid shift toward greater sexual freedom for the unmarried woman, and public acceptance of contraception had helped to remove the stigma of abortion. A woman no longer needed to be reminded for the rest of her life, through the presence of an unwanted child, that she had "transgressed" sexually. An accidental pregnancy for the unmarried or married woman no longer needed to be, as a British physician called it, "a millstone round her middle."

The welfare problem. Welfare rolls were on the increase. The increasing number of illegitimate babies and of babies born to households headed by mothers on relief made many states concerned about the high costs they were shouldering. Only eight months after New York State passed the law permitting abortion on request, there was a decided decrease in illegitimate births.

Overpopulation. The "population explosion" had become a growing concern for thinking people throughout the world. This grave issue is a matter of sheer survival for all mankind living on this planet. As Maurice Strong, executive director of the United Nations Environment Program, has pointed out, "It took one million years to produce the first billion people. It will take fifteen years to produce the fourth billion." And as a result of the rate at which the United States's population has been accelerating (despite *some* drop in the recent birth rate), Emerson Foote, former chairman of the Campaign to Check the Population Explosion, commented: "The United States will be seriously threatened in less than one generation. Though outright starvation may not face most Americans in the next thirty years, we are already being inconvenienced by water and electricity shortages, telephone breakdowns, increasingly jammed and polluted highways and cities, and the inability of our schools and other institutions to meet the needs of our growing population."

Few private citizens, lawmakers, social scientists, or health groups feel that abortion is the answer to the problem. Yet most agree that voluntary means of stabilizing population that are, as *The New York Times* phrased it, "consistent with human rights and individual conscience" must include a woman's easy access to contraceptives, and if these fail, and a woman so wishes, abortion should be available.

The women's movement. Women's rights organizations put the right to abortion high on their lists of priorities. In line with the move to improve the quality of women's lives (and also the lives of men), to help women fulfill themselves as human beings, not just as bearers of babies, and to give women a choice in the direction of their lives, women's liberation groups declared that a woman can never be completely free until she can call her body her own and have complete control over her procreativity. Groups from various professions agreed with this stand. The Committee on Psychiatry and Law of the Group for the Advancement of Psychiatry had stated: "We believe that a woman should have the right to abort or not just as she has the right to marry or not" (*The Right to Abortion*, Scribner's, 1970).

Medical progress. Many medical advances have been made since the days in which the archaic and outmoded abortion laws were written into the states' law books. At a time when surgery was crude and medically unsafe, and there was a great chance of infection in all surgical operations, the rigidity of these laws helped to protect and preserve the life and health of women. Today this is no longer the case. Tremendous improvements have been made in operative techniques and procedures, and abortion methods are highly sophisticated and safe, particularly during the first three months of pregnancy. The risk of complications is extremely low and the risk of death is minimal when an abortion is performed early, under optimal medical conditions, and by licensed physicians trained in gynecology.

Concern for the unwanted child. One of the most fundamental and crucial issues of all is the position of the *truly* unwanted child. Cases of child neglect, of the battered and abused child, are on the increase. Emotionally neglected children are being raised in rich and poor homes that are not really homes at all. Unwanted children fill not only our foster homes and orphanages during their growing years but often our jails and mental hospitals during their adulthood. An unwanted child is deprived of his birthright: motherly devotion and the tender, loving care of at least one parent. And this nurturing is a must if he is to become a mature human being and a responsible citizen. Motherhood now can be a matter of choice, not of calamity. The

Group for the Advancement of Psychiatry has stated in the report already quoted: "There can be nothing more destructive to a child's spirit than being unwanted and there are few things as disruptive to a woman's spirit than being forced into motherhood without love or need."

A much better and more peaceful world may be possible if every child born into it is planned for, wanted, and loved.

Abortion Laws as They Now Stand

The United States Supreme Court has ruled that:

- Until approximately the end of the first twelve weeks of pregnancy, abortion is a decision that rests between a woman and her physician.

- During the next twelve weeks, "the State, in promoting its interest" in the woman's health, may, if it so chooses, impose regulations on the abortion procedures in ways that will safeguard her health.

- After this time, "the State, in promoting its interest in the potentiality of human life, may, if it chooses, regulate" and even prohibit abortion ex-

25

cept when it is necessary to preserve the mother's life or health.

Furthermore, the decision abolishes all residency requirements; a woman who wishes to have an abortion may do so in any state in which she happens to be.

Any doctor or assisting person has the right to refuse to perform an abortion should it go against his religious or moral principles. Some doctors willingly perform an early abortion but refuse to proceed with an abortion after about the twentieth week of pregnancy. There are reasons for this reservation. Sometimes it is difficult for an obstetrician to tell within two weeks, one way or the other, what stage of pregnancy a woman is in, particularly if the woman herself does not know, or has falsified the date. The other reason for hesitation is that after the twentieth week a fetus may possibly survive outside the mother's womb—although rarely. Nevertheless, under the Court ruling such an abortion can be performed regardless of the time span if a genetic defect has been discovered or if there is any serious threat to a woman's health or life.

As a result of the Court's decision, facilities will be established all over the country to meet the predicted rise in abortions. Some of these facilities may not meet the standards which will be set up eventually by the states, hopefully in full cooperation with local and state

26

health departments and medical societies. The importance of finding a suitable and safe abortion clinic or hospital whose doctors are well trained in abortion techniques cannot be too strongly emphasized.

The anti-abortion fight may continue, as there are powerful groups who oppose this great social reform. While every woman has a right to refuse to abort if it is against her religious or moral beliefs, the loud and dramatic protests of the anti-abortion groups should not frighten the woman who does wish to terminate her pregnancy, nor should they intensify or reinforce any guilt she may feel.

2

Making the Decision

You fear, you suspect, or you know you are pregnant. You have skipped a period, maybe two—or more. Whether married or single, you feel that a baby at this time in your life would be catastrophic for you and for others concerned. Feeling trapped and desperate you may decide that an abortion is the only way out. Or you are doubtful and uncertain—even terrified at the thought of going through the whole procedure. Women in this situation often move from one decision to another, and then back again. Some, reluctant to face the unpleasant situation, decide to put it out of their minds for a while and see what happens.

Should you be in this spot, *do not wait*. You cannot afford to think about it "tomorrow." You must think about it *today*. For, if after learning more about the facts and feelings involved in having an abortion, you decide to end your pregnancy, you must act swiftly, yet with caution. It cannot be emphasized too strongly that *the earlier* a woman has an abortion, the easier it will be for her physically, emotionally, and financially. But for the moment, try to set aside your emotions, your misgivings, and your impulse to "do something." Instead, sort out some facts and feeling.

Don'ts

Before deciding what to do, there are some things you must *not* do. Since time is of the essence, it should not be wasted by trying out gymnastics, useless pills, witches' brews, or do-it-yourself remedies.

Surprisingly, in this day of advanced and widely publicized medical knowledge, and despite the fact that abortion is now legal, some women still try shortcuts. Through following dangerous "remedies"—part of the unshakable folklore handed down from generation to generation—they hope to avoid all the expense, red tape, pain, fear, conflicts, and emotional upheaval associated with medical abortion. Quite a number of these women arrive at hospitals and doctors' offices hemorrhaging, seriously infected, and sometimes tragically injured.

Gymnastics. Do not try high jumps, broad jumps, jumping off tables or down a flight of stairs. The fetus rests in an almost impervious shock-proof container within the abdominal wall, and then within the wall of the uterus, and furthermore, within a sac of fluid which protects it from outer pressures.

You cannot dislodge the embryo or fetus this way, but you can dislodge some bones.

Witches' brews. Do not believe for a minute that by taking "purges" of castor oil, ergot, quinine, and the like you will unhinge the fetus. Quinine can cause cramps, nausea, and other unpleasant symptoms. It may cure malaria, but it cannot "cure" pregnancy.

Douches with detergents, vinegar, clorox, lysol, or other searing chemicals will not end your pregnancy—but they may end your good health.

Drugstore remedies. Do not let a fraudulent druggist sell you a Magic Pill to make you unpregnant. You will lose your money—not your pregnancy.

The same applies to pills that are sometimes prescribed by doctors. If you are *not* pregnant, they may bring on a menstrual period, but if you *are* pregnant, the pills will not remove the pregnancy.

What about the "morning-after pill" taken shortly after exposure to pregnancy?

This "pill" consists of strong doses of an estrogen hormone, diethylstilbestrol (DES), taken by mouth or through injection over a period of four to five days beginning within seventy-two hours after intercourse. Few women can take this strong dosage without vomiting up most of it. Although the Food and Drug Administration has approved the use of the drug for "emergency" situations (after unprotected sexual intercourse), at the time of this writing the drug remains highly controversial. Some doctors are using it with apparent success; others will not use it because they consider that research is still inconclusive. But some are optimistic about other "morning-after" medications now in early stages of experimentation.

In any case, you are too late for this pill if you have missed your period.

Instruments of torture. Rubber or plastic tubes still find their way up the uterus, as do knitting needles, wire coat hangers, celery stalks, and whatever else a panicky woman can find.

The latest misfortune in do-it-yourself gynecology is an instrument that women (particularly on the West Coast) devise, distribute, and use on one another and on themselves. The device is patterned after the "Karman cannula," which cannot be sold except to trained professionals. The cannula is a thin plastic tube attached to a syringe, which is worked up into the uterus and slowly rotated. In less than a minute, it draws out the menstrual lining and the fertilized (or unfertilized) egg. This technique, when used by a gynecologist, is called menstrual extraction, menstrual aspiration, early aspiration, endometrial aspiration, or menstrual regulation; it can be used successfully only within five days to about two weeks after a missed period.

Medical opinion is at present divided about the merits of gynecologists' use of this technique. Some doctors feel that it has value as an occasional "emergency" treatment. Others will not use it at all and are waiting for further controlled observations. Some say that when it is performed on a nonpregnant woman it does not result in a true physiological menstrual period, but that the resultant staining and bleeding differ from the usual menstrual flow. If performed on a pregnant woman, it is nothing more or less than an early abortion. In the words of Dr. Alan Guttmacher, director of the Planned Parenthood Federation of America, ". . . anybody who attempts to do it herself is courting disaster."

Any attempt at self-induced abortion can result in a badly infected or perforated uterus, sometimes with tragic results.

Are You Really Pregnant?

There is always that chance that this "pregnancy" is a false alarm. The chances are slim, but they must not be overlooked. Often a woman can't remember just when she had her last menstrual period, particularly if her periods are irregular. Besides, emotional upsets, tensions, and strains can push the period way out of kilter for days—even weeks. So can a change of climate. Drugs such as LSD, certain barbiturates and amphetamines, and heavy tranquilizers can play havoc with the menstrual cycle.

If a woman is sure that her diaphragm, intrauterine device, or other contraceptive "slipped," or if she was off the pill, or remembers that neither she nor her partner used any contraceptive, she may jump to rapid conclusions. She may then be right—or wrong.

Do not be misled and sigh with relief if some slight bleeding or staining occurs around the time of the first or second missed period. A woman can well be pregnant and still have what seem to be light periods for the first few months of pregnancy. However, there may be other symptoms of pregnancy such as nausea, a fullness in the breasts, a frequent need to urinate, a sudden change of appetite, extreme fatigue, or an inability to sleep at night. But emotions can play a role here.

The human organism is a complex structure. The

mind and body are interrelated, and the emotions often play strange tricks. Extreme worry, fear, and unconscious emotions can bring on symptoms such as morning sickness and breast fullness. The only way to be sure is to have a pregnancy test.

In arranging for a pregnancy test, avoid the counsel of anyone who says, "I know someone who . . ." unless that someone happens to be a reputable physician. There is many an unscrupulous "doctor" who will gladly diagnose a woman as pregnant even if she isn't —and will then perform an "abortion" on her for whatever sum he can extract.

The married woman who has already borne a child probably knows how to obtain her pregnancy test, and the married woman with a first pregnancy should have no problems either. An "emancipated minor"—one who is married, or living away from home and self-supporting, or living at home but paying her overhead —will, by and large, have no difficulties in getting her test. The "unemancipated minor" may run into roadblocks.

A girl who is under age (fifteen to twenty-one, depending on the state), living with her parents, or living away from them but dependent upon them financially is at times at the mercy of certain laws that have nothing at all to do with a woman's right to have an abortion. These laws are related to the question of a minor's rights to medical care without parental consent. Some states deny this right to a teenager, some grant it, and others have fuzzy "exceptions." In a state where this privilege is denied, a girl may find that hospitals, clinics, and doctors will refuse to examine her or give her the standard urine test without her parents' consent. This means that the unfortunate girl has to involve her parents before she even knows definitely that she is pregnant. One of the reasons for this situation is that medical people fear malpractice suits which can be brought against them by irate parents.

But the girl need not despair. Although the law in some states may seem to be entirely against her, there may still be legal ways for her to get help. If she calls the nearest office of the Planned Parenthood Federation or the Clergy Consultation Service on Abortion, she will be put in touch with someone who can advise her about her legal rights and who will give her moral support throughout her ordeal, whether it is the ordeal of telling her parents or that of finding a way to get the necessary tests and to take whatever course of action the tests indicate to be necessary. (See the Foreword for guidance in locating these organizations.)

The pregnancy test. A urine sample is required—the first early morning specimen is best. It can be put into a plastic bottle and brought to the clinic, hospital, laboratory, or agency. Some clinics and facilities can do this

35

"prognostican" test in about two minutes. Others take a couple of hours.

The very best time to take this urine test is two weeks after the first skipped menstrual period. If it is taken earlier it may well come out negative (meaning no pregnancy), even though the woman may actually be pregnant. To be certain, the test should be repeated one week later.

If the test is positive, the next step is to find a reputable gynecologist (your own doctor can refer you to one) for a pelvic examination to determine how far along you are in your pregnancy.

Sometimes a woman bypasses the urine test after having skipped two full periods when she "knows" quite rationally that she is pregnant. Then she goes directly to the clinic, hospital, or doctor for her examination.

Do You Really Want an Abortion?

With all doubts removed as to your physical condition, there are a number of things you may want to consider, as the termination of a pregnancy is not always the answer for everyone. (For a consideration of alternatives, see Chapter 6.) Before deciding on an abortion it

36

might be helpful to get a closer look at some of the many different feelings which may accompany the decision. These feelings concern you, your family, and the father of your child, whether he is your husband or another man. Some basic emotions are the same for both married and unmarried women, but some emotions and some aspects of the situation are different.

The Married Woman

The advent of a woman's first pregnancy usually affects the deepest part of her feminine self. Consciously or unconsciously, her pregnancy may be to her the final affirmation of her femininity and an identification with her mother: she, the daughter, can also create a child.

But for many married women, along with the initial pride come certain doubts. Even those couples who carefully planned for a baby find themselves saying: "Can we really afford this baby just now?" "Where will we *put* the baby?" "Am I ready for parenthood?" "There goes my career!" "Now we are really trapped!" For most couples these doubts soon disappear and husband and wife begin to look forward to having their child. The woman begins to have fantasies about her forthcoming baby: she wonders what sex it will be, thinks of different names for it, imagines holding it in her arms, dreams about what it will look like, contemplates its future. But recent studies have found that the woman whose pregnancy spells real hardship or disaster usually inhibits these fantasies and may deny she ever had any. For such a woman, the first negative thoughts about the fetus within her do not disappear but are further compounded by feelings of gloom and despair. Most of the woman's psychic energy then is turned outward—toward the immediate problem of how and where to get an abortion.

When a married woman knows her pregnancy can be legitimately brought to an end, her feelings of relief cannot be underestimated. Yet feelings are not always clear cut. For a large number of women the decision to abort is not easily arrived at—no matter how badly they need to take this step. Simone de Beauvoir, in *The Second Sex* (Knopf, 1953), describes the woman who, "in her heart . . . often repudiates the interruption of a pregnancy which she is seeking to obtain. She is divided against herself."

Whether a woman feels she has enough children already—two or four or eight—or whether this pregnancy has followed the last one too rapidly, down deep she may possibly feel torn, despite her firm conviction and relief that she need not be forced into going along with this unwanted pregnancy. "I feel as if I'd been rescued from drowning," sighed a mother of four. "Maybe now I can really take care of the needs of the children I've got. But it's a tough decision anyway."

A mother may be drained physically, emotionally, and financially by childbearing and may suddenly find herself pregnant at a time when other women of her age are going through menopause—or at a time in her life when she wants to get back to, or get started on, a career. Or this pregnancy may be one extra burden in a life that is overwhelmed by other pressures. She may have strongly developed maternal feelings—may have already experienced the joys and tribulations of motherhood and have been a loving and devoted mother to her other children. But she knows that an additional baby would place a heavy burden on herself and on her whole family. Whether she decides to have the baby or to abort, she may feel pangs at knowing she must make this choice.

One woman said, wistfully, "Here I am giving up my unborn baby when so many women can't have children at all." Another woman, with no previous children, put it this way: "It would be nice to have this baby. I wonder what it would be like." Nevertheless she realized that to have the baby she would have to give up her strenuous job as a waitress, and she needed to work while her husband was slowly recovering from a long and serious illness.

A woman may want an abortion because she is not

sure she wants to continue her marriage. Or she may be living through the nightmare of knowing that the father of her unborn baby is not her husband.

Much depends upon how many weeks or months a woman has been pregnant. Usually there is a decided difference between a woman's psychological attitudes in her first weeks of pregnancy and those after she already has experienced changes in her body—weight changes, enlargement of breasts and nipples, stirrings of the fetus in the womb—and has become aware that there now is a growing organism within her. A strong part of her wants to nourish this growing thing into independent life. She may find herself wondering whether it would have been a boy or a girl. Her decision, particularly if she has waited so long that a "salting out" is necessary, may be an emotionally painful one.

Even a woman who does not seem to be experiencing conflicts or doubts or guilt—the one who just wants to get through with the abortion as quickly as possible—usually likes to be reassured that she is not alone. Few women can approach an abortion without misgivings, some of which may be because society's previous attitudes have become deeply ingrained into her personality, despite the fact that the termination of an unwanted pregnancy has become permissible and acceptable as a woman's human right.

40

These uncomfortable, complex, ambivalent feelings are shared by nearly everyone. Recognizing them in yourself may at least help you to come to your decision fully confident that you have weighed all the pros and cons. In the words of a very sensitive mother of three who underwent an abortion: "There were no doubts at all in my mind that this is what I wanted to, and had to do. Yet it was a deeply personal and shaking experience. By having come to grips with my feelings, however, I feel much freer."

A woman seeking to end her pregnancy should talk over her situation whenever possible with a skilled professional counselor: her own doctor, a social worker, a marriage counselor, a clergyman, a psychologist, or a psychiatrist. An unbiased, emotionally uninvolved outsider can help a woman determine whether her decision to abort is based on her own desires or someone else's coercion.

A trained counselor will not try to persuade a woman one way or another. The counselor acts as a sympathetic and understanding sounding board, to help her get a clearer view of all that is involved in an abortion, help her examine her true feelings, and assist her in coming to her *own* decision.

A very young married couple were both working toward college degrees, living in a cramped off-campus room, holding part-time jobs at minimal wages to support themselves. On a particularly warm and lovely spring day, the couple decided to drive out into the country for a picnic, and in a moment of joy and abandon they made love—taking no contraceptive precautions whatsoever. They were dismayed later to discover that "just this once" had resulted in a pregnancy. They were particularly upset because both had recently experimented with LSD. It would not only have been a great burden and hardship to add a baby to their responsibilities, but they were worried about the possible effects of the drugs upon the fetus. And, as they said to the clergyman whose counsel they sought, "We aren't emotionally ready for a child. We both feel this is not the right time for us to become parents." The clergyman, after exploring the situation with them, helped them arrange an immediate abortion.

A woman went to an abortion clinic at a hospital after having had a fight with her husband at breakfast. In keeping with the policy of the hospital, she was advised to take a few days' "cooling off" time and to discuss her problems with a social worker. Having had this opportunity to review her feelings, the wife came to see that her decision had been made in haste and anger. She went through her pregnancy serene and happy.

The widow or divorcée who becomes pregnant after the death or divorce of her husband is, obviously, in the same situation as a pregnant unmarried woman—unless she has growing children, in which case her situation is much, much worse. Not only is she concerned about caring for the other children during this new complication in her life, and worried about its emotional effect on them—but if her ex-husband is still alive he may have the right to take the other children away from her.

The husband's feelings. Sometimes a woman seems to have little voice in this very personal matter concerning herself and lets herself be persuaded into an abortion by a husband or parent. Down deep the woman may really have a need for the baby. If she terminates her pregnancy against her deeper feelings, she is more likely to experience guilt or remorse afterward.

A widow in her late thirties with two adolescent children married a divorcé who also had older children. When she became pregnant, her husband was adamant about not wanting any more offspring. As she later admitted, "He pushed me into this abortion." Soon after the abortion, her husband died and her depression upon his death included much anger and bitterness for having been deprived of the child she had longed for. "I wanted his baby so much. He took away what would have been mine and his, and now I have nothing of him."

Some husbands, however, may have quite different feelings. The idea of abortion may be totally in opposition to a man's ethical or religious standards. Or a man may think his wife is rejecting *him* when she rejects his unborn child. One father of three daughters, hoping for a son, was keenly disappointed in his wife's decision to abort. An abortion may even arouse in the husband fears, not always conscious, that he has in some way injured his wife, that he is at fault, or that she may be injured by the experience itself.

Whether his reasons for anxiety seem rational or not, the husband should be involved in a session with the professional counselor or with the obstetrician. He should go along with his wife unless he prefers to go alone. In a good marital relationship, except in special circumstances, the decision ought to be a mutual one.

The Unmarried Woman

Sometimes an unmarried woman doesn't really understand why she became pregnant—why her contraceptive method "failed" or why she neglected to take precautions. Her "reasons" for becoming pregnant are sometimes quite complex and lie beneath the surface of her mind. They cannot and need not be dredged up at this moment because there are more immediate and pressing problems to consider.

Frequently a pregnancy occurs in a relationship between a man and a woman who truly care for one another but who feel they are not yet ready for the responsibilities or the permanent ties involved in marriage. In such a relationship, the man is usually supportive.

The public image of the casual, promiscuous seducer —that "no good Charlie"—or the young man who was just "sowing his wild oats" and got caught was never a true or realistic one and today is even less so.

Rather, the young man is likely to offer the young woman moral support, to accompany her to the clinic or hospital if he can, and if he is able, to help her with the expenses. One seventeen-year-old boy gave this touching note to his sixteen-year-old girl as she boarded the train from a small Midwest town to a city hospital: "If I could scrape up the money or leave my job I'd come with you, but I want you to know that I will be there with you in spirit every minute of the way."

At other times a girl or woman is very much alone in her distress either because she does not know which of several men made her pregnant or because she and the man have broken off the relationship. Sometimes she does not want to have anything more to do with the man or even to have him know of the pregnancy. The pregnancy may have occurred as a result of a random sexual encounter, or even when the woman was under the influence of alcohol or another drug.

The man's feelings. One of the most hurtful experiences a woman can have is to try to bind herself to her partner permanently by becoming pregnant, and then to have him fail her by refusing marriage. She feels she had been loving and giving and now she is "losing" not only her baby but the man too. Many women who have had a good steady relationship with a man are shocked when his first words on being informed of the pregnancy are, "For God's sake, get an abortion!"

The woman's reaction is likely to be that the man is rejecting her. She thinks that he does not love her, since she has always assumed that "if a man 'gets you into trouble' but really loves you, he'll marry you."

An awareness of a man's conflicts and emotions will enable a woman to understand his reactions. While a man may act one way on the "outside," he may be suffering in his own way on the "inside."

Naturally, a man's individual reaction will depend on his background and on his earliest experiences with his mother, father, brothers, and sisters, even though he may not consciously remember these earlier years.

A man may feel guilty for several reasons. While he may be proud on one level that he was able to impreg-

46

nate a woman—because it boosts his masculine pride, his "machismo"—he may also feel frightened. If the girl was a virgin he may feel he has damaged her. He may feel strongly down deep within himself that he has a responsibility, that maybe he should be bolder and assume this responsibility by taking full care of the woman and the child. He feels perhaps that he is "copping out." He too may wonder what the baby would have been like if we had kept it? Whether or not they are fully aware of it, some men feel quite frustrated in denying themselves fatherhood.

For these and other reasons, even though it is the woman who has to go through with the abortion, she should try not to judge the man too harshly if he fails to be as sympathetic or responsive as she would like. The experience is likely to have shaken him deeply, too.

The Unemancipated Minor

The young girl living at home—especially if she is underage—faces a difficult, sometimes an intolerable, situation. Repeatedly, girls pour out their anguish to others: "But I *can't* tell my parents. They'd kill me," or "They'd throw me out." Another frequent comment is "My father (or mother) has heart trouble; this would finish him (or her)." Often a girl will exclaim, "My mother is going through emotional troubles, you know;

47

she is in her menopause and I'm afraid of what this would do to her."

Realistically, everyone knows that the days of "Never darken my door again" are long since gone. Parents are not likely to banish their daughters from home. To be sure, parents may be angry, may rant and rave, may be hysterical, shout, weep. They may be hurt, bewildered, ashamed, confused, self-accusatory, stunned. And when all the emotion has died down, they (or he or she) will in most cases be "with" you, support you, and what is even more important, get you the best help that is available.

For a girl in her teens, the incident is sure to be a maturing one, to say the least. Part of the maturing experience is the realization that her parents have been shocked, angry, and hurt and are likely to feel that they have failed as parents. It is hard for mothers and fathers to recognize that their daughter is a sexually mature young woman who can bear children, and not the innocent virgin they would like to believe she is. The girl may feel that she has failed her parents, and this can cut even deeper if she has the kind of parents who hide their disappointment and hurt and quietly rally around her.

Fortunately, there are also advanced and realistic parents who are quite aware that a pregnancy can occur in the lives of their unmarried daughters.

One girl ran all over the small town in which she lived to find someone who would give her an abortion, and nearly got into the hands of a quack. Her own father happened to be a highly skilled, much respected and loved local doctor. Finally, trembling in fear, she told him of her situation. Quite calmly, without even involving the girl's mother, who was highly emotional, the father made proper arrangements for the abortion.

In the long run, each family is unique and no one can really "tell" a girl what she *must* do. Sometimes communication has been so seriously blocked off since childhood that the young woman feels she just cannot unburden herself to her parents. In addition, there may be special problems involved that make it impossible for her to confide in them. Yet in spite of difficulties within a family, this kind of crisis can often bring about a new and better family relationship.

Where to Go for Abortion Referral

Avoid the commercial, profit-making abortion referral agencies which advertise their services. Such agencies are a booming business—or racket. Sometimes the agency gets a kickback from the clinic it refers you to; sometimes it will charge you a large amount of money just to refer you to a hospital; sometimes the exorbitant fee includes the price of the abortion, but there is no way of knowing how much the agency's cut will be.

The information you need can be obtained without charge from either the Planned Parenthood Federation or the National Clergy Consultation Service on Abortion. (See Foreword for ways to discover the office nearest you.) Telephone to make an appointment for an interview. At the interview you will be able to discuss the problem, and if your decision is to go ahead with the abortion, you will be given a referral to the proper facility. The Clergy Consultation Service will ask you for a letter from your doctor confirming your pregnancy and indicating when the pregnancy occurred; this is to guide the clergyman in selecting the medical facility to which to refer you.

Even after you have signed up at a clinic or hospital, you can still change your mind about the abortion. No one is going to force you to go through with it because you have made an appointment. But if you do decide to back out, be sure to let the clinic or hospital know promptly so that your cancelled appointment can be given to someone else.

3

Having the Abortion

When you have definitely decided that you want to
end your pregnancy, you may begin to have some un-
easy feelings about "what they do."

It is the unknown, the strange, the imagined fears
that threaten us most. Abortion, with its long history of
hush-hush, still seems to many like some mysterious
and unmentionable punishment meted out to those
who "go against nature" or whatever our cultural my-
thology has tried to make us believe. (For that matter,
any surgical intervention "goes against nature.")

Many people still have a mental image of a dark and
dirty back room where some hack abortionist or quack
doctor carried out his gruesome operation when abortions were illegal. Or thoughts drift to the publicity

given to the occasional mishap—which can also occur in a safe and legal abortion—when a woman died, possibly for a reason not even directly related to the abortion. Undeniably, an occasional mishap *does* occur during abortion, just as in any surgical situation, even in childbirth—where the risks are even greater than in legal abortion. But newspapers play up disaster for all it is worth, and you "remember."

Fears can arise from lack of knowledge of what really takes place, from bits and pieces of unrelated information, or from complete misinformation. Once you understand what actually takes place, your fear and anxiety can be greatly lessened and you will be more able to cope, because at least you know what you have to cope with.

While procedures differ from place to place within specific application, there are four basic methods in common use today. Two of them are indicated when the pregnancy has not exceeded about twelve weeks from the last menstrual period (LMP). The other two are used when the woman is in a later stage of pregnancy.

Abortion Early in Pregnancy

Dilatation and curettage (D&C). This is a procedure which is also used for medical reasons other than abortion. When a woman tells friends that she had to go to the hospital for a D&C these friends have no way of knowing whether or not she was having an early abortion.

If you are going to have a D&C to terminate your pregnancy, you may find that some hospitals require you to check in the night before and stay overnight following the operation. However, more and more hospitals and private clinics are doing D&Cs on an outpatient basis. A D&C can be performed under general anesthesia, either by inhalation or by an injection of sodium pentathol into the arm; it can also be done under local anesthesia.

If your doctor has decided to use a local anesthetic, which means that you will be aware of what is happening, you may want to know what to expect. Unless you have had a recent pelvic examination, that is the first part of the procedure, and if this is your first experience of a "pelvic," you may, in spite of having had sexual intercourse, feel embarrassed, awkward, and helpless in the position you have to take. You usually change into a hospital gown and then climb onto an examination table similar to the one in any doctor's office. The doctor asks you to raise your knees and put your feet into the stirrups placed near the end of the table. *No one holds or ties you down.* As you lie on your back, the lower section of your body is covered with some sheeting. (Later, during the abortion, other sheeting will be drawn high over supports so you will not see what is happening, although the doctor may describe what he is doing.) The doctor may ask you to slide down further toward him and to spread your knees apart—and your first instinct may be to draw your knees together. Try not to, because things will go more smoothly and rapidly if you can relax, which of course is easier said than done. However, you may already have been given a sedative, possibly with pain-reducing properties. This medication usually does much of the relaxing for you and helps you to cooperate with the doctor.

The doctor will cover his hand with a surgical rubber glove, grease the glove with some lubricant, and then gently insert his fingers into your vagina, exploring the pubic area and carefully pressing your abdomen with his other hand. Through this examination he is able to judge even more accurately what stage of pregnancy you are in.

You may now sense the insertion of an instrument that feels rather cold to the skin. This instrument is called a speculum and it painlessly separates the lips and walls of the vagina so the doctor can see the cervix —the part of the uterus that extends into the vagina. Next, you are given a local anesthetic on the side of the cervix (called a paracervical block) that is something like a Novocain shot given by a dentist. The doctor

54

carefully proceeds to widen the mouth of the womb and the cervix by inserting and then withdrawing a series of narrow blunt rods, each one slightly wider than the next. This procedure is called dilatation. When the opening is wide enough (about the width of a man's thumb), a long spoon-shaped instrument with a hole in the center of the spoon part is inserted and the doctor delicately scrapes out the contents of the pregnant womb. This is the curettage.

The whole process usually takes about twenty minutes.

Dilatation and vacuum aspiration. This technique, also referred to as suction curettage or uterine aspiration, or by other similar terms, is much newer than D&C. Until recently it was used primarily in the People's Republic of China (where it was developed) and in some eastern European countries. It is now the most widely used abortion procedure in the United States and may replace D&Cs entirely. It is swifter— sometimes taking only five or ten minutes—and the loss of blood is minimal. The procedure, like the D&C, may begin with a pelvic examination, followed by dilatation of the cervix but less dilatation than in a D&C. Then, instead of scraping the walls of the uterus, the doctor inserts a small plastic or metal tube connected with a plastic hose, and the contents of the pregnant womb are pumped out by a vacuum apparatus.

After the abortion, a woman may feel a little dizzy and groggy from lying down on her back, and from the local anesthetic or analgesic. Hospitals and clinics have facilities where a woman can lie down and nap or rest. Sometimes coffee and other refreshments are served in a lounge; this is usually a waiting room where relatives or friends may stay. (In any abortion, the patient should have a relative or friend with her when this is at all possible.) After she feels stronger (the time differs for each woman—averaging about four hours) she is sent home, usually with medication and instructions for aftercare.

Trust the physician to know what method he thinks is best for you and with which he is most familiar. Clearly, this need not prevent you from asking him questions beforehand and discussing with him which particular method he intends to use and why he thinks this method is indicated for you. The same applies to questions regarding anesthesia.

Abortion Later in Pregnancy

As with many others who have had difficulties in resolving conflicts about aborting, you may have postponed the decision to end your pregnancy and find that you now are beyond the twelfth week. Or, as occasionally happens, due to irregular menses you were not aware of your pregnant condition earlier. On occasion, too, it is only in the later stages of pregnancy that an obstetrician is able to detect some complications: trouble with the fetus, or perhaps some medical problem with the mother. Under these circumstances a saline induction, or "salting out," may be indicated.

Unfortunately, there may still be some further delay. When a woman has passed her twelfth week the vacuum aspiration method is unlikely to be workable or safe and a D&C may no longer be safe or advisable, and a salting out cannot be performed until a woman is at least fifteen or sixteen weeks pregnant. For technical medical reasons, the uterus and the amniotic fluid surrounding the fetus are not ready for a salting out before that time.

Naturally, the postponement may increase the woman's anxiety. During the interim it is not uncommon for her to change her mind and decide that she will go through with her pregnancy after all.

The salting-out method. The woman, at the hospital, may be given a local anesthetic in her abdomen, though some doctors do not consider this necessary. A needle, inserted through the abdomen into the uterus, withdraws most of the amniotic fluid which surrounds the fetus. The fluid that is withdrawn is replaced by a salt and water solution (or in some cases by a sugar solution). About four to forty-eight hours later, labor begins. Following one or two hours of cramps due to the contractions of the uterus, the fetus and then the placenta are expelled. Sometimes labor is artificially induced after injections of still another drug (pitocin), in which case the emptying of the uterus proceeds much earlier.

More often than not, a woman will be kept in the hospital from the beginning of the injections until the end of the process, which can mean a hospital stay of a couple of days or longer. Other hospitals send a woman home after she has had her injections, with instructions to return *immediately* upon any signs of labor; cramps (which are labor pains), breaking of waters, or any symptoms or sensations that seem unusual to her. Regrettably, not all hospitals make the instructions clear and not all women follow the instructions even when they are clear. There is then the possibility that delivery of the fetus and afterbirth may occur at home, or in a hotel or rooming house, perhaps when the woman is alone and without proper care. Afterward, she must bring the fetus and placenta to the hospital. Such an experience can be extremely upsetting, to say the least. Fortunately, this complication is not likely to occur, because a hospital will usually telephone to check on the woman's condition if she does not return. Out-patient salting out is not favorably regarded by many doctors.

The medical staff at some hospitals is quite aware of the psychological implications of salting out and often gives the patient drugs and anesthetics when labor begins that will keep her from being aware of both labor and the expelling of the fetus.

Hysterotomy. Sometimes the salting-out process is not effective or is not medically indicated. In this event, a woman is brought into the operating room and given full anesthesia, then an incision is made in her abdomen and in her uterus. This incision is called hysterotomy and, as in a Caesarian operation, the fetus is removed. (Hysterotomy is not to be confused with hysterectomy, in which the uterus is removed.) The woman stays in the hospital for several days following the operation. Sometimes, any future babies may have to be delivered by Caesarian section, but this is not necessarily the case.

Fears

Because they are so anxious to have their abortions over with and are afraid that if they do ask questions they will be discouraged from having an abortion, some women never come out into the open with their worries. But as one sensitive obstetrician observed, "By just looking at the strained and tense faces, you know what they must be going through." Other women openly express some of their doubts and fears. The questions that follow are some of those most commonly asked of counselors, social workers, nurses, and doctors.

Will there be much pain? Everyone has his own threshold of pain. This means that, under similar circumstances, some people feel more pain than others do. The pain that goes with a vacuum-aspiration abortion is very brief and mild for most women, and in the early abortion procedures the doctor will tell you when it may hurt. Most of the pain, which takes the form of mild or severe cramps, is in dilatation and much of the cramps come *after* the procedure.

Being sensitive or insensitive to pain does not mean that you are either a better or worse, stronger or weaker, person. The ability to withstand pain depends upon many factors over which a person has little control.

Can anything terrible happen? Patients often ask: "Why do I have to sign that scary paper?" They are referring to the consent paper which every patient who enters a hospital or clinic for surgical intervention of any kind is obliged to sign. What it means, in effect, is that if there are any complications ("unfavorable results," as the paper reads) and suit is brought against the hospital, the doctors and other staff members can show that the procedure was performed with the consent of the patient, who was fully aware of possible risks. To be sure, the paper is frightening in its implications, but it must be recognized that any surgery involves some risk.

As for the questionnaire you may be given, or the questions you are asked: for your own protection, welfare, and safety, answer truthfully. Be absolutely candid about your medical history. Questions about whether you have an allergic reaction to penicillin or anything else, have had difficulty in response to Novocain, have had previous operations or abortions, are anemic—and anything else that concerns your health—must be answered honestly. The answers will not deprive you of your abortion. They may show that certain extra precautions need to be taken, or perhaps that another method of abortion should be substituted for the one that was originally planned. Your honesty will reduce the risks of the procedure you are undergoing.

In a study of 70,000 abortion records conducted by the Population Council Biomedical Division, it was found that only one out of every 200 women who had abortions within the first three months of pregnancy had major complications.

Will there be much blood? In a D&C the blood loss in normal cases is usually less than half a pint—less than what one gives to a blood bank. (Some recent research indicates that bleeding is somewhat greater under general anesthesia because the anesthetic prevents contractions of the uterus, and those contractions tend to prevent blood loss.) There is even less blood loss in the vacuum-aspiration method—an average of about one ounce for pregnancies of eight to ten weeks—about what is usually lost during a normal menstrual period.

In any case, the patient is not likely to see any blood. Should hemorrhaging occur, hospitals have all the standard emergency equipment needed, and a good licensed clinic should also have sufficient equipment and staff to deal with this rare emergency. Accredited hospital-affiliated free-standing clinics are generally located close enough to a hospital that, if necessary, the patient can be taken to the hospital without delay.

Fear of anesthetics. A patient who is fearful of either kind of anesthetic will have a chance to notify the doctor of her fears, either directly or through a social worker, medical assistant, or nurse. Some hospitals and clinics have group discussions about abortion procedures, conducted by either a nurse or a social worker, with a doctor as an occasional speaker. Private patients are able to ask their questions and express their fears with their own doctors.

Does abortion affect future ability to have babies? An abortion performed by a competent physician under safe and hygienic conditions is not likely to affect a woman's reproductive capacity. Nevertheless, this fear does lie deep in the hearts of many women, especially those who have not yet given birth to a baby. Underlying these fears is the longing for a future child under happier circumstances; sometimes there are some guilt feelings too.

Of course, if there has been an infection (through venereal disease, self-abortion attempts, or unskilled previous abortion experiences) that has reached the fallopian tubes, where the egg is fertilized, or if the uterus has been damaged—unusual conditions under the proper medical care—infertility may result. It has been found that repeated abortions tend to weaken the cervix—as does bearing a number of children. Many women who have had repeated abortions are susceptible to "spontaneous abortion," or miscarriage, in which the womb voluntarily expels its contents. In Japan, and in some other countries where abortion serves as a form of birth control, a high incidence has been noted of premature births, with some accompanying risk of problems associated with prematurity.

Attitudes of Hospital Personnel

No one can give an accurate prediction of how doctors and nurses are going to act toward each individual patient. At a good hospital you will certainly get the best of medical care. The chances are high that the medical team will respect your dignity, preserve your self-esteem, and give you emotional support, but this is not always the case, even now. Today more and more hospital staffs are becoming supportive, humane, and kind with their abortion patients. As one married woman commented, after expecting the worst, "They really treat us here as if we were 'normal'." An unmarried woman put it this way, "They don't act as if we had done something wrong. They respect us as decent human beings."

One needs to realize that even after legislational reforms are made—and generally the social climate and attitudes must have changed in order to make such reforms possible—individual, personal, emotional attitudes are slow to change. As in the case of civil rights, where some injustices continue even after laws to prevent them have been passed, on abortion rights there will be those who continue to drag their feet.

A doctor or nurse, for personal reasons, has the right to refuse to participate in an abortion when abortion goes against his or her principles and beliefs. Yet sometimes an obstetrician or obstetrical nurse *does* perform the task put before him or her despite some reluctance. As one doctor coolly stated, "We are public servants and must do what the public wants." However, doctors

64

and nurses may find it difficult to perform in a way that is opposed to their previous training. Unwittingly, then, their true feelings and underlying attitudes may come through, despite efforts to the contrary.

The chances are good that an abortion patient will be handled with kindness and compassion rather than with a judgmental or punitive approach. But until more hospital personnel are trained to view abortion in a new light, as a public health need as well as a human need and an individual right, some uptight responses may still be encountered. One eighteen-year-old revealed that the obstetrician who performed her abortion had said to her angrily, "You should never have gotten into this rotten mess!" And, as she later told her counselor, "His words upset me more than the abortion itself." A nurse scolded a young woman coming in for her second abortion: "What! *You* here again?"

If by chance you are subjected to a caustic remark or any other indication of hostility, try to remind yourself that this doctor or nurse does not even know you. Since the remark is not directed at you personally, there is no need to feel guilty. An abortion is your right and privilege. It is the hostile response that calls for changing.

In all fairness, it must be pointed out that there is another side to this coin. There are times when the hospital staff is really put upon by angry, hostile, excited patients and are at a loss to know how to handle them.

Whatever your feelings may be toward the man who made you pregnant, or your parents, or yourself, try not to provoke those who are trying to help you. Often the staff's job is a thankless one. An angry woman needing and wanting an abortion may still feel that no one is doing her a favor, and may feel unconsciously that she is being harmed or punished. This is one reason that a woman has much to gain by having some counseling before her abortion.

Abortion Clinics

Abortion clinics are springing up all over the United States and it is to be hoped that health departments and medical societies in every state and local community will be setting up their own health standards.

The sole purpose of a fully licensed free-standing abortion clinic (that is, a clinic either affiliated with a hospital nearby, or a licensed nonaffiliated clinic equipped with emergency apparatus) is to provide a woman with a medically safe early abortion. Consequently, the personnel of such a clinic is most likely to be extremely sensitive and responsive to the girl or woman who comes through its doors. In a number of these clinics, the medical assistant or counselor may be a registered nurse, but she may just have a degree in psychology or social work—or she may have no degree at all. In a number of clinics she is selected for the job chiefly because of her concern for people and her understanding of the complex feelings and responses an abortion can awaken. Her empathy is often due in part to the fact that she has had an abortion herself. All the assistants are trained to handle the various medical tasks and psychological concerns related to abortion.

Preceding the abortion, the patient is usually given a questionnaire to fill out on her medical history, and sometimes she is asked questions about her fears, doubts, and other feelings associated with the abortion. She may be asked how she became pregnant (contraception or none), and about her relationship with the man. In at least one clinic, the patient has an option to omit her last name on the questionnaire but is asked to leave a telephone number at which she can be contacted. This is required so that if she is remiss in returning the post-abortion questionnaire she can be reached by telephone for follow-up.

In all accredited clinics, the patient receives a medical check-up, which may include a pelvic examination, though this may be given later. After the check-up, if the clinic provides counseling, she and her counselor talk together informally about her feelings (in many clinics this counseling takes place through group discussions) concerning the abortion, the man who impregnated her, and even about his feelings, if he knows about the abortion. The counselor then explains in simple language what will take place during the abortion. In some clinics, the assistant remains with the patient throughout the entire abortion procedure, and may talk to her or hold her hand if the patient wishes this.

Contraceptive advice and instruction is given to each patient in addition to a medical instruction sheet. Besides this, she may be given a "hot line" telephone number—one which a physician will answer at any hour of the day or night for any physical or psychological problems that might arise. This service is usually included in the price of the abortion.

Costs

The costs of abortions vary from one community to another and from one hospital or clinic to another. If a woman is on welfare or is covered by Medicaid, Blue Cross, or any other insurance plan, the abortion may be paid for like any other medical expense. But coverage varies, and a woman should check with her doctor and her insurance agent before making any commitments.

In some cases, a woman is charged according to her ability to pay. For information about the prevailing rates in your own community, call the nearest Planned

Parenthood affiliate or National Clergy Consultation Service branch. (See Foreword.) According to the Clergy Consultation Service, the *average* fee for an early abortion should be about $125, and a later, in-hospital abortion should average about $350.

4

After the Abortion

Aftercare at Home

The abortion is over and done with. Intensely relieved, you would like to forget the whole thing as quickly as possible. But it is not likely that you will be able to forget about it yet, since there are some very important medical aftercare instructions you will need to follow. Besides, it is quite possible that you may find yourself reacting with some unexpected moods and emotions.

The clinic or hospital will probably have given you some aftercare instructions for use at home. For your present and future health do precisely what has been suggested. Should you not have received such instructions, or should you be rather vague about what *was* suggested, here are some of the major precautions:

- Take it easy for a few days. Get lots of rest. Avoid lifting and bending. Your body has gone through a number of abrupt changes and needs time to readjust.

- If you have been given pills to minimize bleeding and prevent infection, take them faithfully. Some doctors recommend multiple vitamin pills and iron pills until all bleeding has stopped. Try to eat well-balanced meals.

- Bleeding can be expected for a few days, even for ten days or longer. However, if bleeding is excessive (more than with a heavy menstrual flow) or if it lasts more than two weeks, get in touch with the hospital or clinic, or with the doctor who performed the abortion.

- Cramps can also be expected for the first few days. If they seem excessive, get in touch with the facility or with the doctor who performed the abortion. Do not take aspirin or any other pain-killer until you have spoken to some medical authority—telling the truth about your abortion.

- If you are feverish and the fever is over 100 de-

71

grees, *immediately* contact the same medical person or facility. The fever may be caused by infection, and you must not delay in determining its cause.

- Nothing should enter your vagina until you have had your postabortion checkup with a doctor. No baths (showers are O.K.), no douches (unless prescribed), no tampons (sanitary napkins are O.K.), and no sex.

- Call the doctor if you notice any unpleasant-smelling vaginal discharge.

- Have a medical checkup with an obstetrician-gynecologist two to four weeks after the abortion.

- About four to six weeks after the abortion, menstruation may start again. Some doctors say that two to six weeks after the abortion you can begin to take birth control pills (if this is the kind of contraception that has been advised for you and if it is what you are planning to use).

- If you notice other postoperative symptoms—of any kind—report them immediately to the clinic, hospital, or doctor.

Unfortunately, many women who have abortions out of their own communities fail to report back to the hospitals, clinics, or doctors who took care of them. The doctors then are unable to know whether or not their patients had that very important two- to four-week medical checkup. The medical staff often remains totally ignorant about how their patients fared after the abortions, physically or emotionally. Women are often truant about returning to the hospitals or clinics even in their own communities. Feeling well, they believe a checkup is unnecessary. Even though you may have valid reasons, such as distance, for not returning to the place where you had your abortion, do seek a good gynecologist in your own community and follow through with a postabortion examination. (If you are under age, you should again get in touch with the person or persons who took care of your referral and who will follow up with you now.) This checkup is vital for your present and future health as well as for your future ability to bear children.

Emotional Reactions

After you have had a tooth pulled, you receive sympathy and comfort from your family and friends. After you have had an operation, you usually receive get-well cards, flowers, presents, and lots of attention, sympathy, and comforting. What is more, you can talk about it all freely. By describing in detail just what happened you can help rid yourself of some of the unpleasant effects of the experience.

When a woman has had an abortion she is not apt to receive such consolation. She may not want to talk about her experience to anyone. This may be due in part to the moralistic attitudes toward abortion that still prevail in certain communities today—despite the fact that abortions are now legal. Or it may be because she feels that this experience has been a deeply personal and private one. In either case, she may feel rather alone with it all.

A girl's close friends—particularly among college communities or in other groups where women are living or working together—often do rally around her supportively, and this support can be very helpful. If you are living alone and are fortunate enough to have at least one good friend or understanding relative in whom you can confide—or, if you are a very young woman, some trusted older person—by all means "let it out" if you can. You may feel soothed, comforted, and restored emotionally by having been able to unburden yourself—instead of going along with everything bottled up within. Of course if you are a married woman, your husband is likely to give you this support.

Relief. Generally, a woman's first and strongest emotional response is that of release and relief. She feels she is lucky to be out of an unhappy situation. In many instances a woman begins to take stock of herself and of her life style. Some typical reactions: "I have grown so much emotionally through this crisis in my life." "I see and understand myself better now." "I do not regret this experience because now I am able to face life more realistically." "While I hope I never have to go through an abortion again, and I can sleep nights now, I still feel I have truly learned about the value and meaning of life. I not only understand myself much better now but I am more tolerant of others. I have a better sense of where to go from here."

Guilt. It is not easy to predict how any particular woman will react to an abortion. Some go through the experience with little or no emotional upheaval. Their entire response seems to be that of relief and little else. Others have mixed emotions, experiencing some relief but also some guilt or depression, which may persist for a varying length of time. "It still is painful to think about it," one woman said months afterward. "It's like a bad dream that repeats itself."

People respond differently to crises, as they do to pain; some more sensitively, others less so. How you react is no reflection on your character. Whether or not

75

a woman feels upset, whether she sails through the experience smoothly or finds the course rough, her individual reactions do not indicate either strength or weakness. A good deal depends on the woman's age and on why she became pregnant. Much depends upon the attitudes of those who assisted in the abortion, the woman's familial, ethnic, and religious background, her ingrained attitudes, and other influences. Finally, it is obvious that the earlier in the pregnancy a woman has an abortion, the less likely she is to feel upset about it.

A young unmarried woman, who had her abortion in her twelfth week of pregnancy, and who had shown no visible signs of pregnancy prior to the abortion, which was performed over a weekend, projected some of her guilt feelings this way. When she returned to work on Monday morning after the abortion, she was certain her straitlaced boss knew what she had been up to. She began to worry about what would happen to her job if he "found out." The problem was imaginary, since she was the key person in her department and ranked high in her boss's estimation. Besides, abortion was now legal. Another unmarried woman had the same reaction as the girl quoted in Chapter 1: "People look at me in such a queer way, as if they knew what I had done."

A married mother of three near-adolescent children said, after a salting-out abortion: "I just cannot look at babies these days. I feel just awful and weepy when I do."

The signal lights have turned green. The legality of abortion has now been confirmed by the United States Supreme Court. Why then do many women still attach some stigma to abortion and experience unwarranted guilt?

A number of psychiatrists suggest that some of the guilt has been built in by society and is now deeply rooted in the unconscious mind. People of the Western world have inherited a value system based on the interpretation of the Judeo-Christian ethic which holds that you destroy a life even when you destroy a living sex cell. Attitudes cannot be changed overnight—sometimes not even in a generation.

Consciously and intellectually we may reject this attitude as nonsense—impractical, unrealistic, and certainly outmoded in today's world and under the new Supreme Court decision. But the unconscious mind does not always go along with rational thinking and sometimes punishes us in subtle, unrecognizable ways.

For example, if a woman has been brought up to feel that sex is "dirty" or "bad," even though she realizes consciously this attitude is ridiculous, she may feel deep within her that abortion "serves her right" and is a just

77

punishment for her transgression. This reasoning may even apply to the promiscuous girl and to the girl who has sex with seeming abandon. In subtle ways, as with the woman who could not look at a baby without feeling uncomfortable, a message comes through from the deepest part of the mind, causing guilt feelings.

A girl may feel she has failed herself somehow by having become pregnant and that she deserves punishment for her failure. Furthermore, many women have strong maternal desires, which now have not only been thwarted but stamped out consciously. In addition, women are generally brought up to believe they should want to be mothers—even though many may not want motherhood at all.

If a woman has been treated with humanity and warm concern by the hospital or clinic staff and if she is fortunate enough to receive the same understanding when she returns home, her possible guilt feelings may be greatly reduced. But if she has been subjected to sarcastic remarks or other evidence of a condemning attitude, her feelings of culpability may be reinforced.

A woman who has needed a salting-out abortion is likely to have been especially subjected to anxiety and other psychic pain and needs tremendous understanding and moral encouragement by kindly and sympathetic assistants who are aware of her ordeal.

Some psychiatrists feel that since laws against abortion have been declared unconstitutional, the moral implications will be largely eliminated, and with the passage of time both the stigma and the unconscious guilt will be considerably minimized.

Depression. Many women tend to feel weepy, sensitive, depressed, and let down after the abortion. These feelings may last a few days, or sometimes longer. Occasionally a woman may have a delayed reaction. Everything seems to be fine and under control for days, weeks, or even months after the abortion, when suddenly, around the time the baby would have been born, the woman becomes depressed. The unconscious mind often has a way of keeping score.

Remarks like these are common: "I cry at the slightest thing these days." "I often have to run out of the room and go and cry somewhere." "I feel so sad." "I know I have lost something. I feel as if I had given part of me away."

Even when a woman has had a strictly therapeutic abortion—one performed for the sake of her life or health, or because the fetus would have developed into a baby with a severe mental or physical defect—she is often left feeling sad.

Psychiatrists and obstetricians interpret these feelings in several ways.

A few days after the birth of a baby, many women go through the "maternity blues" or "baby blues." These

79

may last for a day or for several days. Postabortion feelings may be somewhat similar. They are, in part, a response to separation shared by all of us when we lose a person or thing that has been close to us. And what can be closer, in a primitive sense, than the relationship of a woman to the growing fetus inside of her? It stands to reason that the longer a woman carries the fetus, the more difficult the parting will be.

One psychiatrist points out: "Whenever surgery is performed in which some body part is removed—be it a useless appendix or an aching tooth, or whatever—the person is often subject to an accompanying sense of deprivation and loss." The same psychiatrist suggests that the pregnant woman's parting with her fetus may unconsciously revive memories of a separation from, or the loss of, a much loved person from an earlier period in her life.

There are doctors who strongly believe that the abrupt hormonal changes that influence these moods also play an important part in postabortion responses. Other doctors point out that many women do not experience the "baby blues" after childbirth, although they too go through the same hormonal changes. There may be factors connected with the "let-down" feelings that are still unknown.

A woman who feels let down after giving birth to her baby may revive in spirits when she begins to form a new and different relationship with her newborn, whereas the woman who has lost her fetus may have just the emptiness—albeit a great sense of relief.

Maybe all of the foregoing seems pretty heavy going and hard to take—and has little to do with *you*. You may reject all these responses as utter nonsense. But if these descriptions do ring a bell somewhere, you are not alone. There are countless quite normal women who have these temporary upsets.

If you continue to feel depressed, guilt-ridden, or upset for more than a few weeks, you would be doing yourself a good turn by getting in touch with a family counselor, a social worker, a clergyman trained in counseling, or a psychiatrist. In some cases, a woman's continued depressed feelings and self-reproach have little or nothing to do with her abortion. The abortion itself may have brought to the surface conflicts and troubles that were unresolved and had their origin long before pregnancy. By getting help you may also get a new lease on life.

Relationships with Other People

An unpleasant experience can often turn out to be a blessing in disguise—drawing out unsuspected inner strengths and bringing about deeper self-awareness

81

and a sense of mastery. An abortion may well be such an experience. It often alters a girl's relationship with her family and may deepen a woman's relationship with her lover or husband.

A nineteen-year-old college girl who had been living for some time with a graduate student of twenty-one said, "We have grown together through this experience. It has brought us so much closer and put us in real contact with each other. We had felt practically married before but had taken things for granted. But now we know how important it is for a child to be really wanted and needed and to be born into a stable home. We are sure that we will be able to make it—and soon."

Family members who previously had difficulty in communicating often find new ways of reaching each other. One seventeen-year-old told of her new relationship with her parents. "My parents did so much for me. I know now that no matter whatever happens to me in life, I will always be able to count on them if I need them."

Another girl began to see her mother in a new light. "I am no longer afraid of Mom. I realize now how much she loves me and cares about my welfare." Still another young girl admitted, "The hardest part of my experience was the feeling that I had shocked and hurt my parents. But it broke down the walls that had been built up between us. We now are able to share in per-

sonal, frank, and open discussions." Others will tell of
how much more intimate they became in all their personal relationships. "I no longer feel shut off, lonely,
and afraid. I feel freer."

Other young women, not so lucky, have to muddle
along somehow within the same unsatisfactory family
relationships as before. "My only fear," some say, "is
that my parents will someday learn the truth about
what happened to me."

A Spartan attitude does not help resolve a situation.
When home relationships continue to be difficult and
emotionally disturbing, discussing the situation with a
trained counselor will take part of the load off your
shoulders.

When a woman had hoped that the man who got her
pregnant would marry her and he does not do so, or
when she is abandoned completely by her man, the
disappointment sometimes makes her wary of all men.
Some women become embittered and determine to ab-
stain from sex. Others find they have real problems
with sexual responsiveness, partly, perhaps, because
they have fears of becoming pregnant again. But the
temporary frigidity may be a form of self-punishment
of which the woman is unaware, or it may be a defense
against becoming emotionally involved again.

There may be other reasons for these difficulties, but

by and large when a woman finds herself happy and relaxed again in a new and trusting relationship—one in which she has not jumped quickly on the rebound—her momentary sexual revulsions, inhibitions, and hangups disappear.

For those who have learned more about themselves and about the proper use of contraceptives, sex may take on a new and clearer dimension. One young woman described her feelings in this way: "I realize now that sex is not all fun and games but involves responsibility between two people and a real caring relationship." Another unmarried woman noted that before her abortion sex had just been an extension of her own needs. She and her lovers had merely used each other selfishly to satisfy themselves sexually with little regard for each other as individuals. After her abortion she commented, "I have now found the proper place for sex and love in my life."

People who have counseling often discover that they have been using sexual relations for the channeling of all kinds of feelings that have little to do with sex. Granted that the sex drive is present, other pressing needs can be discharged through sexual relations: hostility toward the opposite sex, feelings of helplessness and dependency, needs for power, escape from loneliness, proof of femininity or masculinity, the need to be thought of as lovable and desirable, the need to escape

84

from boredom, and sheer curiosity. Under such circumstances, contraception is likely to be ignored or incorrectly used, and pregnancy and the need for abortion often follow.

"When I meet a new man or fall in love with someone should I tell him about my abortion?"

This question comes up frequently in postabortion interviews. There is no single answer, as much depends on how the woman herself views the experience. Was it very upsetting—one that will leave memories for a long time? Or was it one about which the woman has little or no feeling? She may feel it is something that should be shared with a person who becomes an important part of her life, or it may be of no special significance to her and therefore why (or why not) tell someone she loves about it? Or she may feel the experience to be very private and therefore nobody's business.

The liberated woman may well feel that in today's world premarital sex is a woman's privilege just as it is a man's privilege and that a terminated pregnancy is part of that privilege. She might feel that if a man accepts the fact that he is not the first man with whom she has gone to bed, he should be able to accept the fact that she has been pregnant by another man. Her reasoning might be: If he is not able to take this admission, he is likely to be narrow and rigid in other views of life and therefore good riddance to him.

One woman in her late twenties exclaimed vehemently: "I couldn't keep secrets from any man I loved. I would be miserable!" Yet many people who are very much in love do not care to tell or hear about previous sexual experiences. Such confessions often arouse uncomfortable and resentful feelings in both parties. "But supposing," one may ask, "he finds out?"

A woman might also want to consider whether her need to tell the man reflects a need to remove her own sense of culpability. She may be trying to use him as her confessor or therapist. She may truly feel that no relationship of any value can be based on lies, believing that a firm and valued relationship must be based on mutual respect, trust, understanding, and acceptance. But she can also ask herself whether it really *is* a lie not to tell everything about one's life.

Another point to consider is whether the man's background was one in which abortion was considered a crime or sin, in which case the admission could be very disturbing to him. A woman might then wonder whether she would be justified in making him come face to face with an unpleasant reality, particularly if her pregnancy had resulted from a random sexual experience of no importance to her. Certainly, if a woman felt she had to "reveal all" she might be discreet enough to wait at least until the relationship had ripened and become secure enough to test out—if she felt that the relationship needed such testing out.

The only advice anyone could give a woman—unless she discusses the problem in detail with a counselor—is "Play it by ear." Each woman must determine for herself, on the basis of her own feelings and her knowledge of the man she loves, whether she would be hurting him—and herself—more by telling or by not telling. Only you can decide what is right for you.

The Repeater

With modern techniques of contraception, there usually is no good reason for a woman to have to repeat her unpleasant experience. As the following chapter explains, an understanding of the correct use of various contraceptive methods and of their psychological and social meanings will help a couple choose the method that is best for them.

While some less sophisticated cultures still use abortion as a method of population control, in our society it is *not* an alternative form of contraception. It is a "back-up measure," an escape hatch, and a last resort when all else has failed.

Nevertheless, some women return time and time

again to a hospital or clinic with an unwanted pregnancy and a desire to abort again. Sometimes they go to a different clinic or hospital and do not admit to their previous abortion or abortions.

It is understandable how a woman can get caught twice in a row—or later once again. She may not have used any contraceptives the first time for a variety of reasons; a second time her method may not have been the right one for her; and perhaps after having had a baby, she may not have realized that her contraceptive was no longer adapted to her.

Sometimes a married woman wants another abortion because of serious marital problems. Perhaps her husband has deserted her just after she became pregnant; or a second marriage has proved unsatisfactory and she wants to terminate her pregnancy and get a divorce.

Many women, afraid to use birth-control pills because of alarming press reports or forbidden them because of medical contraindications, neglect to seek out alternative preventive measures. And some women simply play Russian roulette: "It can't happen to me this time."

Repeated abortions do not usually come about by accident. If a woman repeatedly becomes pregnant and repeatedly returns for abortion, there must be some inner motivation for her abortion pattern. Something is making her "accident prone."

A look beneath the surface of the mind of the repeater who *has* been given contraceptive advice and information but will not use it often reveals surprising
facts. The woman is motivated by strong irrational
forces of which she is unaware. The "reasons behind
the reasons" both for repeated pregnancy and for the
desire to interrupt it are interwoven.

Some of the unconscious reasons are:

- The need to break away from an unhappy home
  situation and from parents in that home.

- The need to bind a lover more closely to her. This
  may be an attempt to compensate for a loss—of
  a former lover, of a parent (usually the father)—
  or even of a job.

- A need for punishment and self-injury to atone
  for guilt feelings, possibly connected with having
  had sexual relations.

- A need to discharge hostility—against herself, her
  husband or lover, or the unborn child, or to "get
  even" with her own mother or father for some
  real or imagined injury or lack of love.

- A need to test the love of her father or mother.

- Feelings of loneliness and emptiness. The fetus
  inside of her helps to fill this void and makes her

feel complete. But she cannot follow through with the pregnancy because she feels unable to take care of herself and therefore to take care of a child.

- Lack of self-esteem. The sense of worthlessness may be alleviated by pregnancy, since this condition gives her a temporary feeling of being valuable. But when she again becomes aware of the changes in her body, she realizes that she is unable to assume the responsibility that is demanded of a mother.

Whatever the reasons, the repeater is usually in serious need of psychiatric assistance. She needs to be made aware of what her repeated self-destructive behavior means to her and helped to face the future more realistically.

5

Contraception

Truths about Birth Control

Some women become pregnant because they use no birth control method at all or failed to use it "that once," and you may have been one of them. You may have used a method you heard about, only to find upon becoming pregnant that it was not a contraceptive method at all. Or you perhaps used a reliable method faithfully but incorrectly, or used a method faithfully and correctly and found that it failed you.

Despite the highly publicized information that is available on contraception, for many the subject still remains veiled in mystery and misinformation. Some people think of contraception as a grim chore, an added

91

expense, a big nuisance, an obscure threat to bodily health, or an unpleasant interference with the joys of sexual relations, depriving sex of its spontaneity.

These objections have little validity. Contraception, thoughtfully planned and carried out, is a benefit and even a necessity. Relaxed and freed from the tension created by fearing that any act of sex may result in an unwanted pregnancy, a man and woman may find themselves experiencing even greater sexual and emotional fulfillment.

Nothing in life comes absolutely free. There is always some price—and not in money alone. And there is no one hundred percent guarantee. There are some minor inconveniences with the proper use of almost any contraceptive, but the cost is slight compared to the psychological, physical, and financial cost of an abortion.

It is advisable to consider the pros and cons of each method so that you may choose the one most appropriate and effective for you and your partner, hopefully with the approval of a doctor or clinic. While medical safety and security are the primary considerations, some other factors need to be considered:

- A person's social, religious, ethnic, or national background has an important bearing on the choice of a birth control technique. Each woman must select the method most acceptable for her and her partner.

• The comfort of both partners must be assured.

• Some methods are more effective than others, but even the safest methods are not safe unless used *consistently, carefully,* and *regularly.* (Read all the small print on the directions.)

• The chances for effective birth control are increased by the strong wish of both partners to prevent conception. Ambivalence contributes to laxities of one kind or another, and then you wonder why you were "caught."

• "Back fence" advice is sure to be misleading. Your friends' or neighbors' bedroom lives, psychological needs, sexual drives, and marital relationships are apt to be quite different from yours— no matter what they tell you. Gynecologists, as well as counselors at Planned Parenthood and Family Planning clinics, are trained to make allowances for these differences.

• The more a man and woman are able to plan their lives thoughtfully and realistically, the more they are able to communicate and cooperate with each other as real partners, the more sensitive they are to each other's needs—the more successful they are likely to be with contraception.

- Birth control is a mutual concern. If either partner states or implies by attitude "it is up to you," the results are apt to be disappointing. The underlying hostility of such a stance is bound to cause "accidents."

Contraception for the Unmarried Woman

A single woman who has just terminated an unwanted pregnancy needs to be especially realistic about precautions for the future.

When a woman meets a new man, she may quite naturally consider, if only in the back of her mind, the possibility of having sexual relations with him. But the sexual confrontation may take place at a time when you both had meant merely to kiss and fondle each other. Suddenly and unexpectedly, overwhelmed by strong physical urges, and in the heat of the moment, the fear of pregnancy may fade away or be ignored in the belief that "it can't happen again so soon."

This is something of a dilemma. It may seem expensive and foolish for a woman to take daily pills when her sex life may be only sporadic. Or she may feel guilty about being always "ready" with a permanent intrauterine device or an inserted diaphragm, fearing that such preparation is an open admission that she intended to have sex. Or she may feel that contraception "spoils the romance," spoils the "beautiful spontaneity" of lovemaking.

This illusion is a dangerous one to cherish. An unwanted pregnancy is a *high* price to pay for "spontaneity." Why should a woman be unwilling to admit to herself or to her partner that she is prepared, if and when the moment arrives? Sex is a normal part of life. There is no need for a woman to think less of herself for being practical and responsible, or to fear that her partner will think less of her for being so. He may be mature enough to want to protect his partner by wearing a condom until both have decided to continue with the relationship, at which point the woman may want to use a contraceptive regularly.

The fact that a woman is prepared does not mean she must have intercourse with any man who wishes it. She need not let herself be exploited or used. If she places value on herself and on her body she will not share herself until she is sure that she has found someone she really wants.

She may even find she has more control over her sex life if she is able to postpone and wait—a sign of growth and maturity. Although modern life plays up instant sex and the "need" for constant sex, there is no reason for a woman to feel deprived if she is not having sex all the time. Moreover, a woman who does not want sex except under very special conditions does not need to feel that her attitude is abnormal. A woman who wishes to avoid sexual intimacy until she is sure of herself and of her man, however, is wise to keep away from alcohol, drugs, or any situation in which she "finds it hard to stop."

The Safest Methods

The pill. When taken exactly as prescribed, the pill (oral contraceptive) assures virtually 100 percent protection against pregnancy.

The pill contains certain hormones which usually prevent the ovaries from producing an egg (ovum) each month. With no egg for the male sperm to fertilize, no pregnancy can take place. The new low-dosage pill—also referred to as the minipill—does not consistently suppress ovulation, but it works anyway. The actual mechanism of contraception of this new pill is not known for certain. Some doctors believe that it may temporarily interfere with other mechanisms in the female reproductive system.

The pill is usually taken daily from the fifth day after the beginning of the menstrual period for twenty days or so. (The time varies for some of the newer pills—the physician's instructions should be followed carefully.) Then for five days no pills are taken. One to three days after stopping the pill, a light menstrual flow will occur, and on the fifth day after it starts, the woman begins taking a new packet of pills.

All a woman needs is the ability to count. No mathematical genius is required. Some packets of pills even help the counting by providing calendar numbers under each pill for the days of the cycle. Others simplify the counting by including five other pills which contain iron or some harmless substitute so that the woman can continue to take a pill every day until the packet is empty. Some doctors recommend brands that allow for seven pill-less or substitute pill days.

If you forget to take your pill one day, it is urgent that one be taken at the very moment you "remember you forgot to remember"—even if it means taking two pills that day. If you have been a dropout for more than one day, doctors advise continuing the pill as usual and adding another contraceptive method for the remainder of the month.

The pill is not usually guaranteed as effective until at least seven days after the first pill is taken. Some doctors say that another additional protective method should be used for the first two weeks to one month after having started to take the pill; after that the pill is sufficient.

There are many myths about the pill. Some of them stem from unfounded, sometimes unconscious, fears some people have about taking any kind of pills, which they believe can "poison" the system. Other myths come from distortions and exaggerations by the popular press of careful scientific studies which indicate under what particular circumstances it is inadvisable to take the pill. The pill is contraindicated for about 5 percent of women. Since 1959 over 9 million women in the United States have been using the pill, and it is still considered safe *when taken under proper medical supervision.*

Sometimes there are side effects, positive and negative. Many women who previously had painful menstrual periods or premenstrual tensions no longer experience these discomforts after taking the pill. The bleeding may be very light and last just two or three days. Some women, however, on first taking the pill may feel nausea, have tender aching breasts, gain weight, and feel bloated. These symptoms tend to disappear as the body adjusts to the hormones. Since there are thirty-five or more varieties of the pill, the doctors may suggest trying a few different varieties before deciding on the one most suitable for you. If uncomfortable symptoms persist, it may be advisable to find some other type of contraceptive.

A woman who has tendencies toward clot formation or vein inflammation is usually advised by her doctor not to take the pill. Also, a doctor may advise a woman against the pill if she has had liver malfunctions or unexplained vaginal bleeding or may question its use by any woman who has had heart or kidney disease, high blood pressure, diabetes, migraine headaches, or severe mental depressions. However, these conditions do not automatically rule out the pill; the doctor will decide in each individual case.

The pill is definitely contraindicated for those who have had breast or womb cancer. A gynecologist can determine—by a pelvic examination and a "pap smear" —which is painless—whether a woman has any precancerous condition. The pill does not cause cancer, as all the studies on *humans* up to now have indicated. Actually, by having a yearly pap smear taken, a woman on the pill has an automatic cancer checkup. Gynecologists nowadays usually include a pap test when examining a patient for any reason.

Fertility is not affected by the pill. Shortly after discontinuing the pill a woman is as fertile as ever.

The pill costs relatively little: $1.00 to $2.50 for a

month's supply. Some Family Planning clinics and some hospitals dispense them for even less, and sometimes in cases of dire economic need, at no cost at all.

Intrauterine devices. If you do not want to bother with the daily routine of taking the pill or are afraid you will forget to take it regularly, or if it is ruled out for medical reasons, an intrauterine device (IUD) is an excellent solution, provided it is right for you. A woman's chances of becoming pregnant within one year while using an IUD are about 3 percent.

IUDs are plastic or metal objects of varying sizes and shapes which are inserted into the uterus by a gynecologist. They are usually a one-time proposition. A woman does not have to work at this contraceptive method. Once inserted, an IUD will usually stay in place for years, and it is easily removed if she decides to have a baby. All that is necessary is a monthly self check to see that the device is in place. The IUD's string or "tail" dangles slightly from the uterus. A probe with the fingers will determine whether it is still there. Should the device have slipped out—which does happen occasionally—another contraceptive should be used as a temporary stand-in until a visit can be made to the doctor.

If the IUD has been properly inserted, its presence during intercourse is not felt by either the man or the woman.

How do the IUDs work? Doctors themselves are somewhat puzzled about this. IUDs do not interfere with ovulation. Some doctors believe that the device prevents the fertilized egg from becoming implanted into the lining of the uterus. Other theories have been presented but none has been proved.

Many women feel crampy during the time the device is being inserted and for a short time thereafter. Aspirins help this discomfort. Some women experience heavier menstrual flows than before. Usually, the condition returns to normal after a few months. There are women who cannot tolerate an IUD, because of continued difficulties or because the womb expels it. Sometimes, however, all that is needed is an IUD of a different shape or size.

An IUD cannot get "lost" somewhere up in the uterus, as some women imagine. The device is not likely to damage a woman physically. It does not produce cancer and will not affect a woman's fertility or the health of her future baby. Rarely, but it has happened, a woman gives birth to a normal baby despite the fact that the IUD has remained in place throughout the pregnancy.

Occasionally the device may be difficult to insert in a woman who has never given birth, but a gynecologist may recommend one nevertheless.

About 7 million women all over the world and about

2 million women in the United States are now using IUDs. They seem to be becoming increasingly popular as newer and more effective models are being designed.

IUDs are a one-time investment. Costs of the medical examination, insertion, and the device vary according to the doctor, the clinic, and the patient's ability to pay. The average cost at a clinic runs to about $30; a private gynecologist is likely to charge much more, while hospital clinics sometimes charge little or nothing.

If you are using an IUD, do not fail to have a gynecological check up and a pap smear at least once a year.

The diaphragm. The diaphragm is a soft, flexible, round, rubber cuplike disk edged with a bendable but firm rubber ring, that is squeezed into a tampon shape and inserted deep into the vagina. After insertion, it springs back into shape and completely covers the cervix (neck of the womb), blocking any passage of sperm cells.

Before inserting the diaphragm (also called a pessary) one teaspoonful of spermicidal jelly or cream is placed within it, and a bit more is spread around the rim, to kill any sperm that might happen to get by the diaphragm, or that might still be alive when the diaphragm is removed.

A diaphragm is not a contraceptive one can borrow from a friend. It has to be carefully fitted to each woman's own size, by a gynecologist, who then shows the woman exactly how to use it. Periodic checkups are necessary to see if the size and fit are still correct— especially after childbirth or any sizable gain or loss in weight.

Neither partner should be conscious of the pessary during intercourse. It does not affect sexual sensations. If either partner is aware of the device, it is either the wrong size or has been inserted incorrectly. If discomfort continues, it may be necessary to use a specially shaped diaphragm—or to try some other contraceptive method.

Some women worry that they will not be able to insert the diaphragm or get it out easily, or that their long nails will pierce it. The diaphragm is tough and durable and is not likely to tear. One can always place water in it to see if it leaks. Some women worry that they will damage the vagina with their fingernails as they insert the diaphragm. A sketch of the vagina and its surrounding parts is often included with the diaphragm to help those who are not sure about where their cervix is located. And for those who find it unpleasant or difficult to handle their inner parts, a special insertor can be purchased separately. This special insertor is shaped like a curved rod and often conforms to the size of the diaphragm. As it is pushed up into the vagina, a slight twist of the insertor releases the diaphragm into the proper position. The diaphragm can be removed by the same method.

Although a diaphragm can be put in up to six hours before intercourse, many women insert it just before going to bed. If intercourse is attempted more than once during the night, or again early in the morning, extra contraceptive vaginal cream or jelly should be inserted by means of a plastic plunger tube. This plunger can be attached to the jelly tube and the right amount is squeezed into the applicator.

A diaphragm should never be removed until six hours after intercourse, but it can be left in place for about twenty-four hours. A douche—if taken at all—should not be taken until six hours after intercourse.

There is one little emotional hitch for some women. When a woman has inserted her diaphragm at night and no lovemaking is attempted by her partner, the next morning as she removes the contraceptive she may feel a bit hurt and rejected. This is of course more likely if communication between a couple is not free and easy. A woman who feels this way might feel hurt and rejected in any case. Some women prefer to insert the contraceptive when the very first sexual advance—

verbal, nonverbal, or tactile—is made, or when mutual signals have been exchanged. This interruption of the follow-through should take less than three minutes (after the trick of inserting the device has been mastered).

A nuisance, to be sure—but less so than an abortion.

Before the pill and the IUDs came along, the diaphragm was the most popular method of contraception. It has about a 96 percent chance of success. When it does fail it is usually because no spermicidal jelly or cream was used with it, or because a second intercourse took place without a new application of jelly or cream, or because it was not carefully fitted or inserted—or because it was not inserted at all!

The condom. The condom (also called a rubber or a prophylactic) is one of the most widely used contraceptive methods, in which the man assumes the responsibility for pregnancy prevention. Condoms serve a double purpose—since they are highly effective as protection against venereal disease—more so against gonorrhea than syphilis.

Condoms are readily available in drugstores and do not require a doctor's prescription. In some states they are also available from vending machines in bars, bus stations, and gambling casinos. The most reliable condoms are made of very strong but thin latex, and cost

about a dollar for a package of three. Good-quality condoms are more likely to be obtained from drugstores
than from vending machines.

Condoms offer a fairly high degree of protection
when certain precautionary measures are taken:

- A man does not enter his partner's vagina before
  putting on the condom. This is important because
  the lubricating fluid that emerges from the penis
  during sexual excitement—before ejaculation—is
  often loaded with sperm cells and the delay in
  using a condom after insertion increases the
  chances of pregnancy.

- Spermicidal jelly or cream or foam (*not* vaseline
  or cold cream, which can cause rubber deteriora-
  tion) should be distributed over the condom once
  it is on, to reduce the possibility of tearing and
  as a lubricant to ease friction.

- About half an inch or an inch of space should be
  left at the closed end of the condom after it is
  rolled on. This is to prevent an air pocket and
  provide room for the semen, thereby reducing the
  amount of stress on the material.

- To prevent the spilling of any sperm into the
  vagina as the man withdraws his penis, he should
  hold onto the rim or ring of the condom.

- Should any unforeseen accident occur (a tear in the condom, for example—and for security's sake the condom can be tested after withdrawal by filling it with water under some pressure to see that it is leak proof), spermicidal foam, jelly, or cream should be immediately inserted into the vagina.

Some couples are satisfied with this method of preventing pregnancy, others find that the condom interferes with the acme of tactile sensations for both partners, as well as interfering with the feelings of closeness. (Some doctors suggest putting a small amount of spermicidal foam, jelly, or cream *inside* the condom as well as on the outside, since this may increase sexual pleasure for the man.) Still others object to it because they feel it interrupts lovemaking.

There are times when complete, absolute fulfillment may need to be put off—for example, before a couple know and trust each other completely, or when a woman is not otherwise prepared. It is advisable for all married couples to keep a packet of condoms handy in the home for "emergencies," when no other contraception happens to be available at the moment of desired lovemaking.

The Riskier Methods

Spermicidal foams, creams, and jellies. Somewhat further down the list of effective contraceptives come the spermicidal foams, creams, and jellies that need no doctor's prescription and are suggested for those who cannot use any other contraceptive methods or who cannot get to a doctor. Of this group, foams are considered to be the best, but none of these products is as sure as the contraceptives already discussed, and all are best used in conjunction with them.

Special precautionary measures are needed with these, too:

- Products advertised in magazines as "feminine hygiene" are *not* spermicides unless so marked on the package.

- Vaginal foams, jellies, and creams come with instructions as to how much and when to apply. These instructions should be followed to the letter, as a sperm cell can remain alive and active for twenty-four to seventy-two hours after ejaculation and the protective coating on the cervix should be thick enough to last that length of time.

- The application must be made no earlier than one

hour before intercourse; if intercourse is to be repeated, even after a few minutes, another applicator full of spermicide must be used.

Vaginal foaming tablets and vaginal suppositories.
Do not confuse vaginal foaming tablets and vaginal
suppositories with the spermicidal foams, creams, and
jellies. They are far less effective—and far more tricky.
Vaginal foaming tablets must be moistened before they
are used. Then they must be placed quite far up into
the vagina no sooner than one hour before intercourse,
but no later than five minutes before, because they
need this time in which to dissolve. After they have dis-
solved, they spread into a foamy film to block the en-
trance to the cervix.

Vaginal suppositories are not very reliable. They take
even longer than tablets to dissolve—about fifteen minutes. And sometimes they never *do* dissolve.

Both of these contraceptive methods must be repeated in the same way as described for the jellies,
creams, and foams, and if intercourse is repeated, even
after a few minutes, another tablet or suppository must
be inserted and time allowed for it to dissolve: five
minutes for a tablet and fifteen minutes for a suppository.

Douches, if taken at all, should be postponed for at
least six hours after the last intercourse.

Vaginal tablets and suppositories are obtainable at any drugstore without a doctor's prescription.

The rhythm or "safe period" method. Rhythm, or restricting intercourse to the "safe" period, is the only family planning method approved of by the Roman Catholic Church. It is based on the fact that ovulation (the production of an egg from the ovary) takes place only once a month during a four- to five-day period—usually around the middle of the menstrual cycle. If a couple abstains from sexual intercourse during the ovulation period, the chances of pregnancy are minimal.

Since many women do not have regular menstrual cycles, and since those who usually do may find their periods irregular at times because of tensions, anxieties, illness, change of climate, or the use of drugs, a highly complex method of investigation and calculation is needed to ascertain the "safe" period for each woman.

To determine the safe period you do need to be a mathematical genius. It is necessary to keep a record of the dates of the menstrual periods for about eight months to one year. (Medical opinions vary; some doctors say that if a woman is regular in her menstrual periods a three-month record is sufficient.) You also have to keep a daily record of body temperature upon arising each morning. Since a great deal of addition, subtraction, and consulting of charts is involved, the rhythm method is not one a woman can easily undertake on her own. A gynecologist or clinic should be consulted. The Planned Parenthood Federation of America has published a booklet on the rhythm method, called "The Safe Period."

The major disadvantage of the rhythm method is that making love is governed by calendars and charts. It may be permitted at a time a couple are not in the mood for it and ruled out just when they feel most loving and passionate. The rhythm method is still quite risky, although medical experts are working to improve and simplify it.

Withdrawal (coitus interruptus). A man needs to have a tremendous degree of self-control in order to withdraw before ejaculation ("pull out in time"). Even then the chances are that the seminal fluid containing sperm cells may be released into the vaginal canal long before the man has his orgasm. All of this places an enormous amount of responsibility and strain on the male partner, and is frustrating for the woman as well.

When the man withdraws and does not direct the ejaculate away from the woman's genital area, she still can become pregnant. Many a virgin with an unperforated hymen has become pregnant in this way. Even if the man has his orgasm on the outer surrounding area of the vagina, the sperm cells can start to work their way upward toward the inner birth canal.

If pregnancy is to be avoided at all costs, and no other contraceptive is available at the time, perhaps it is wiser to avoid the risk by having orgasm during foreplay.

Non-Methods

Douches. Considering that it takes sperm cells only a few seconds to reach the womb after ejaculation, a woman would need to be a champion sprinter to get to her douche bag in time! Some doctors say that the stream of douche water can propel the semen up the vagina even faster.

Women have been flushing out their vaginas for years in attempts to prevent conception. Those who were successful are considered—according to many medical experts—to have been quite lucky, or perhaps they had intercourse unknowingly during "safe" periods, or maybe they just happened not to be very fertile. Douches are not recommended for preventing conception. This includes douching with carbonated water or any carbonated drinks, which, contrary to modern old wives' tales will not "do the trick."

Saran Wrap, intercourse in special positions, intercourse during menstrual periods, intercourse during a mother's nursing period. These are not birth control aids but forms of Russian roulette.

Sterilization

Sterilization of the male. Through a fairly simple operation called a vasectomy, which can be performed in a doctor's office under local anesthesia in fifteen to twenty minutes, a man can be made sterile without loss of sexual desire, virility, or sexual performance.

The doctor makes two small incisions (one on each side of the scrotum—the pouch containing the testes, where sperm is manufactured) and then cuts and ties off the two tiny tubes through which sperm is carried and ejected along with seminal fluid at orgasm. Since the seminal fluid itself is not cut off, the man can still ejaculate, but the sperm cells cannot get through. Instead, they are absorbed by the man's body.

Vasectomies seem to be one answer for many couples who have had all the children they want and can care for, but this step should not be taken in haste. A man needs to consider very carefully what would happen if one of his children should die or if he is widowed or divorced and wished to remarry and have more children. Although the operation can sometimes be reversed, less than half the attempts to do so have been successful.

The reversal procedure is more complicated than the original operation, and few doctors are skilled in it.

For these reasons, vasectomy should be considered final and irreversible. Careful counseling is suggested for couples before they decide to go ahead with the procedure. Sometimes a rather reluctant husband is persuaded to have this operation by an enthusiastic and persuasive wife. If a husband has potency problems or worries about his sexual functioning, such an operation could intensify these difficulties.

There has been talk about sperm banks in which a man's sperm could be "frozen" for future use. Should he want to become a father after having had a vasectomy, his wife could then be impregnated by artificial insemination. At the present time, however, there is no guarantee that the stored sperm would be effective.

According to the Association for Voluntary Sterilization, it has been estimated that over 2.7 million American men still in their fertile years have had vasectomies. The association can supply a list of 2,000 or more physicians throughout the country who are skilled at this operation, as well as information on laws, costs, sperm banks, and other details (see Foreword).

Sterilization of the female. A woman can also be rendered sterile by an operation that can be performed at any time. It is called tubal ligation and consists of tying off the Fallopian tubes (the tubes through which the

114

egg would normally travel downward to become embedded in her womb). It is frequently performed at the time that a woman gives birth to a baby. Should she be having a Caesarian section, the obstetrician can cut and tie her Fallopian tubes at the same time. If she has given birth to a baby in the usual way, she can be sterilized approximately twelve to forty-eight hours after delivery. The operation is done under general anesthesia.

There has been a rise in the number of sterilizations performed on women as newer techniques are being developed. One of them, culdoscopy, involves cutting the tubes with a small instrument that is inserted through the vagina (making an abdominal incision unnecessary). The other technique, laparoscopy (also referred to as Band-Aid surgery) requires two tiny incisions in the abdomen; after the tubes are cut or cauterized, the wound is held together by a Band-Aid. The operation, which leaves no scar, can be performed under general or local anesthetic. This method, yet in its beginning stages of development, costs less than the older methods, but it is not yet available everywhere.

Although a woman's tubes have been cut and tied off, she still ovulates and menstruates each month. As with the sperm cell in the male, the egg is absorbed into the body. And, as with the male, she has the same desire for sex after the operation as before it. This operation too is occasionally reversible, but the process is far more complicated; a woman considering sterilization should also give serious thought to its consequences for the future. Techniques are being developed which may make tying off the tubes a completely reversible operation.

Abortion Pills and Injections

Many promising new abortifacients (substances that produce abortion) are on the horizon. Prostaglandins, a group of hormonelike substances now being synthesized, can cause the uterus to contract and dislodge a fertilized egg or cause miscarriage up to the sixth month of pregnancy. At least one of these substances may replace the unsatisfactory "morning after" pill mentioned in Chapter 2. One type may possibly be used as once-a-month contraceptive, and others may turn out to be real morning-after methods in that they will precipitate menstruation shortly after a woman has been exposed to pregnancy—making it possible for a woman to miss her period without ever knowing whether or not she had been pregnant! This of course would eliminate emotional complications, conflicts, and decisions regarding abortion.

Such "contraceptives" may not be available for several years, although it is possible that they may be on the market earlier. Meanwhile women today can be comforted to know that they have at their disposal reliable contraceptives—and should these fail, abortion.

There is still another promise for the future: birth control pills for the male. These are in the form of hormones designed to stop the production of sperm. A rubberlike capsule containing the hormone is injected into the man's arm or buttock and the hormones are released day by day for about a year. Scientists in Brazil, Japan, Finland, and later the United States will be testing the effectiveness of this implanted pill.

In addition, all the reliable known contraceptives for both women and men are constantly being improved both in comfort and effectiveness.

6

Alternatives to Abortion

What if, for a variety of reasons, you were unable to terminate your pregnancy?

Maybe you delayed too long in making up your mind. It might have been too late for an abortion by the vacuum-aspiration method, or by a D&C, and you then decided you just could not go through with a salting out. Perhaps it was also too late to have a salting out or even a hysterotomy. Or doctors may have decided that an abortion would be hazardous to your health. Quite possibly, too, you reversed your decision to abort at an early stage of pregnancy, perhaps for private moral or religious reasons.

If you are married, how are you going to make peace

with yourself or work out some different plans? And if unmarried, where do you go from here?

For the Married Woman

Frequently, the woman who has changed her mind or is forced by circumstances to follow through with her pregnancy may "take it out on herself." She sometimes feels guilty toward her unborn baby, knowing she had wanted to do away with it. She may wonder how can she ever be a good mother to a baby she didn't want—and still does not seem to want. However, there is a vast difference between a truly unwanted baby and a baby who initially seems to his pregnant mother to be unwanted.

Just because a woman rejected the idea of becoming a mother in the beginning does not necessarily mean she will reject her baby when it is born. No matter what angry, hostile, or unhappy thoughts a woman may have entertained during the early weeks or months of pregnancy, she may find herself gradually changing. Many mothers—even those who never contemplated abortion—have felt angry, fearful, and upset upon finding out they were pregnant. As time passed, however, and the baby became more "real"—after they felt life or their bodies changed noticeably and as they

119

began to make plans—a reversal of feeling occurred and they began to look forward to the baby's birth.

Many women fluctuate in their feelings about their babies—in wanting them and then not wanting them—from the time of early pregnancy to its very end. Even during the years of childhood mothers sometimes feel loving and sometimes not so loving. Many a child who was initially unplanned for and unwanted has become the apple of his parents' eyes.

But should you not find yourself feeling maternal at first, do not be discouraged. Your feelings or lack of them may not be connected with the contemplation of abortion. There are many mothers who do not experience instant love when they first see their babies. (And how many women fall in love at first sight with the men they later marry?) In fact, Dr. Kenneth S. Robson, assistant professor of psychiatry at Tufts Medical School, and Dr. Howard A. Moss, a psychologist at the National Institute of Mental Health, have done some interesting research on maternal attitudes. They recently took a look at fifty-four young mothers and found that 34 percent of them had no feelings at all when they first looked at their babies; most of them felt love only six to nine months after their babies were born.

Some mothers experience the first warm response to a baby when feeding him or giving him his first bath.

Others experience tender loving feelings when the baby first smiles. Another might say, "I didn't really get a charge out of Jimmy until he spoke his first words." Don't force it. The chances are high that your feelings will develop in their own good time.

These words may offer little or no consolation to the woman who is still deeply disappointed at not having gone through with the abortion or the one who is facing what seems to be an unbearable situation. You may be widowed, separated, or divorced; your financial position may be such that another child would mean going on welfare; your marriage may be breaking up; the father of this child may be someone other than your husband. In any such circumstances you would be well advised to seek professional counseling on the advisability of adoption. Many married women with "problem pregnancies" are being helped by the guidance offered at a number of adoption agencies. Going to an adoption agency does not necessarily mean deciding to give up the baby. An adoption agency will not try to persuade anyone to give up a child. On the contrary, an agency is often able to work out a plan for keeping the child that the mother might not have thought of by herself. Adoption is suggested only if it truly does seem to be the best solution.

No adoption agency, Family Service Association agency, clergyman trained in counseling, marriage counselor, or psychiatrist will lecture or moralize. People in the family counseling field are generally with it. They are there to help people in difficulty and to spare them unnecessary suffering. No individual situation is new to them. They have seen them all over and over again. Impossible as your situation may seem to you, they can offer you help in coping with it and in finding new and happier ways of facing the future.

For the Unmarried Woman

Three different solutions face the pregnant unmarried woman who does not want to abort: marriage, arranging for the baby's adoption, or keeping the baby.

Marriage

For many centuries couples have rushed into marriage just because the girl discovered she was pregnant. It would be impossible to determine how many people have married for this reason alone. Some had intended to marry "some day"; others are propelled by anxious parents into a "shotgun" marriage. In an earlier era, a young woman who for some reason could not marry the father of her child might marry another suitor, sometimes without telling him of her pregnancy if it had not become evident.

If people marry solely from a need to follow convention, or through a sense of obligation, they are likely to run into some very difficult problems. Marriage can be a bitter hardship when it means curtailment of cherished plans. If a boy still in high school has to give up his dreams of college or professional training and take a job to support a wife and child, he may feel trapped and resentful; a girl who relinquishes plans for college or a career may react in much the same way. Such marriages often have an unhappy ending.

An unwanted husband may be as unwelcome a burden as an unwanted baby. When a girl marries to give her baby a father she has no guarantee that the baby will *have* a father. In some cases she might as well be single because the father is not there emotionally to provide the loving care that is needed.

Both prospective parents will want to consider carefully whether they are willing to give each other and the baby the many years of love and care and responsibility that family life entails. Sadly enough, one of the partners is frequently ready for this responsibility when the other one is not.

If both young parents feel they want to live their lives through together, if they both love *and* like one another and hope for and want a permanent relationship, then there is a good chance their marriage will work out well despite the circumstances. The couple will be providing for the baby's birthright—his parents' enduring love for him.

For people in college it is a familiar sight these days to see a mother coming to classes carrying her baby along with her books. Many couples take turns caring for the baby while they alternate in taking part-time jobs.

If there are practical obstacles to marriage—opposition from parents, refusal or inability of the father to marry, the inability of the girl to locate or identify the father—then the woman is left with only two alternatives: adoption or keeping the baby.

Adoption

Any steps toward adoption should be made through a state-licensed adoption agency, which can be located through a doctor, the state department of social welfare, the Child Welfare League of America, a Family Service Association agency, a clergyman, or the yellow pages of a telephone book under "Social Services."

A licensed adoption agency will provide counseling (free of charge as are all of their services), including practical assistance in planning carefully for the arrival of the baby and for the months after the baby is born.

A woman is not committed to give up her baby just because she has used the services of the agency. Quite the contrary. The social worker there, keenly aware of a woman's conflicting feelings, will not put any pressure on her but will let her take her time to make her decision. The agency workers are deeply concerned and understanding, and know that the decision to give up a baby is one of the most difficult and painful in anyone's life. Many agencies today are giving abortion counseling—they want to be sure that if the adoption decision is made it is the one the woman really feels she needs to make.

The adoption worker will ask the woman about her family background and that of the baby's father, so that they can match these backgrounds as well as possible in trying to find the most suitable home and family for the child. A woman may want a particular kind of home for her baby; if her request is within reason, the agency will do all that is possible to meet her requirements. There are many eager adoptive parents waiting and longing to have a child to love. Because there are many more families waiting to adopt a baby than there are babies available, the agencies are in a position to choose the family who can offer the most in terms of the baby's total well-being and welfare.

Going to an agency will protect the woman from the legal snags which can arise if a baby is given away privately through someone who may "know a married couple who wants a baby."

One young woman concealed her pregnancy from her parents by taking a new job in another city. A doctor there assured her of full medical care and arranged for an adoption with a couple willing to defray all the girl's medical expenses. After the baby was born, the young mother signed papers drawn up by the couple's lawyer. She then returned home telling her parents she had been dissatisfied with her job. Shortly after the baby was born, it was discovered that he was deaf, and the couple refused to go ahead with the adoption. The lawyer called the young woman at home and told her to come for her infant. Had she surrendered her baby to an adoption agency, she would have been legally free of any further responsibility; the agency would have received the infant.

A perfectly healthy baby was born with red hair, which did not happen to conform to the adopting parents' preconceived notions of what they wanted in the child they had "ordered" privately. The mother had to take her baby back.

A couple may change their minds about adopting the baby for other reasons. They may have decided to get a divorce, or the wife may suddenly find herself pregnant, or a number of other circumstances may occur that will cause the prospective baby to be left in the legal hands of its natural mother.

The natural mother learns a great deal through the agency about the adopting parents—their education, financial position, hobbies, personality, religion—but the natural mother and adopting parents never meet or get to know each other's names or identities. Therefore, a mother cannot be tempted to go through the poignant experience of taking a peek at her child at play in a playground, or of hovering around his home, or of one day appearing and declaring her true relationship.

Should a woman have problems about money or wonder where she will live these next months, the agency may be able to give some help and guidance. They may even find the expectant mother a place to live. The agency may help her locate a temporary job, perhaps as a mother's helper or baby sitter.

The agency may suggest a shelter or maternity residence. The number of maternity homes has dwindled considerably since the ban on abortion laws, but they still exist. For some, the maternity home is a real haven. The experience of being with others in the same boat relaxes some women and keeps them from feeling defensive all the time. The expectant mothers in such homes give each other quantities of emotional support.

Others find the mere thought of a maternity residence a nightmare. Shelters are not punitive like jails. In many, a girl may come and go as she wishes, have visits with her boy friend, go home for weekends, or continue her school work.

One of the advantages of going to a shelter is that anonymity is preserved. (Sometimes, but not always, an underage girl may not be able to enter a home without parental consent and financial help. The adoption agency will check on this and similar matters for you.) Staff members will reveal nothing to suspicious or prying relatives and friends. A number of the homes have medical clinics and facilities for the baby's delivery.

Many women decide to give up their babies for adoption and then change their minds; in fact, a woman may change her mind several times during the months of waiting. She may not be ready to make a decision until sometime after the baby's birth. In this event, the agency places the baby in a small foster home where the baby will be given loving care until the mother's *final* decision has been reached. Needless to say, if a woman knows she has to surrender her baby, it is easier on her if she does so shortly after the baby's birth. If, however, there is any chance that with time a mother can work things out and keep the baby, the agency will encourage and help her to accomplish this.

By the time you are asked to sign the release papers surrendering your baby to the agency, you are no longer legally responsible for him nor are you likely to have any legal rights to him. To prevent heartbreak for all parties concerned in an adoption, once the choice has been made to give up the baby, the decision, difficult and painful though it may be, must be regarded as *irrevocable*. The irrevocability will give the baby the start in life which he needs so much: a permanent and stable home and loving parents whom he considers his own. And it will protect the adoptive parents, who will have grown to love the child as their own.

Until six months to a year have elapsed, the new parents continue to have contact with the agency and the agency worker counsels the family to insure a smooth transition. The final adoption papers are then drawn up and processed through a court.

While any mother may feel at once relieved and sad, she should bear in mind the comforting thought that while she is surrendering her baby she is not abandoning him. She is not giving her child *away*, but *into* adoption. She is providing her baby with security, protection, and love. If you have made this decision, remember that you are doing everything possible to assure the baby's welfare and well-being. The agency has carefully selected these parents for your child—parents who sincerely want him and are taking on a task which at this time would be formidable or even impossible for you. Now you can turn to rebuilding your own life. This experience is not the end of the world; it may even be the beginning of a stronger and happier life than you had known before.

Keeping the Baby

Public attitudes toward the unmarried mother are changing rapidly and the stigma attached to unmarried motherhood is lessening, although vestiges of the old-fashioned punitive approach still remain in some communities and within some circles.

At any rate, there is a growing trend in the United States for unmarried mothers to keep their babies. A good number of these mothers live with the fathers of their children, some considering themselves married. As one young woman declared, "What does a piece of paper mean? We are married in the deepest sense, in every way but technically." But the majority of unmarried mothers do not have the financial, emotional, and practical support of a male companion.

The situation may be easier if a woman is a famous, glamorous figure in the performing arts; recently much publicity has been given to actresses and singers who have had their babies without benefit of clergy. Such women, and others who are reasonably well off financially, can afford the complicated arrangements that single motherhood entails. But the life of the average unmarried mother is not so easy or glamorous.

If she is still in high school there is the problem of completing her education. In an increasing number of states, a girl is permitted and encouraged to complete high school while she is pregnant, as well as after her baby is born. About 140 special programs for pregnant teenagers are now under way all over the country. Some schools offer not only regular courses but courses in prenatal care and baby care. A number of the schools are equipped with playpens, cribs, and toys, and sometimes bassinets are lined up right next to the girls' desks! Information about such programs can be obtained through local or state boards of education.

In communities where no such facility is available, schools sometimes send teachers to the home so that a girl can keep up with her work. Other communities have special schools or classes for pregnant girls. And it is always possible for a young mother to pick up her studies from where she left off, after the baby is born.

Parents can usually be enlisted to help with the care of the baby while the mother is completing her education. While this may not always be easy, since it may make the mother feel like a little girl at home again—it still is the best plan if there is no one else close enough to ask. The increased job opportunities opened by a high school diploma make the effort worth while—and will help establish independence. Grandparents can be truly heroic, kind, helpful, and understanding, and can give a baby very special love and care while the mother is away.

A family service agency or an adoption agency (even if you have no intention of giving up your child for adoption) may be of great help in planning a modus operandi and in finding you a job.

After all these initial difficult arrangements and adjustments have been made, the mother may still find it quite an undertaking to work at a full-time job to support herself and her baby. Naturally, she will have to plan for baby care by either finding a good, warm, reliable baby sitter or by involving parents, relatives, friends, or neighbors. She may be fortunate enough to know some other young mother—wed or unwed—with whom she can swap baby-sitting arrangements while working part-time.

To be sure, when a woman returns home from work, exhausted, with no husband there to help or give moral support, it is hard for her to give her baby the time and the patient, warm, tender care that is essential for his physical growth, mental health, and intellectual development. But there are rewards, too, as the child grows, takes on endearing ways, and develops a personality of his own. The path is a rocky one but full of gratification too.

In some communities there are small private boarding homes or nurseries where a mother can leave her baby during the day and pick him up on the way home. Interest in the formation of day care centers for children over the age of two is developing throughout the United States, although not rapidly enough to meet the need. It is wise to be cautious in choosing a day care center. Such a center should either be approved by some accredited social agency or have been formed on an informal basis and run by a group of mothers. A personal visit should be made to see how the school "feels" and whether the children there seem happy. Some of the recently established day care centers are barely more than profit-making parking lots, giving children little of the personal attention they need. Others provide the very best care possible.

In many cities there are Maternal and Infant Care Projects administered by local health departments and sponsored by the United States Children's Bureau, offering medical, social, and educational services for the time before and after the baby is born. Many provide baby-sitting services and facilities as well. Get in touch with your state department of health to see whether there is such a project in your community.

133

The Father's Role

Most men are deeply concerned about what will become of their offspring and therefore should be involved in any decision that is made, whether it is adoption or keeping the baby. It will be very helpful to both if the father accompanies you to a counseling interview or to an adoption agency. If you decide to keep the baby, he should be asked to contribute to its support. It is likely that he will do whatever he can. If, however, there are any doubts about his helping, or if you are reluctant to approach him, it might be a good idea to consult a lawyer. (To find a lawyer, call the Legal Aid Society, which is probably listed in the telephone directory of the nearest large city.) Should the woman apply for welfare, she may be asked to file a complaint against the father in a district attorney's office. If the father has any money, he will be expected to contribute a certain sum each month. If the father's whereabouts are unknown, or if he cannot be traced, or if a woman is not sure who the father is, the welfare department may pay the total amount (depending on welfare allotments in her county and state).

Keeping a baby can be done successfully even under circumstances that look dubious to an outsider. There are good social agencies that will stand behind a woman and assist her in mapping out a plan that can

134

make this decision work out. And some day you may find a man who will love and accept your baby just as he loves and accepts you.

Although there is rarely just one single perfect solution, whatever your decision may be—abortion, marriage, adoption, or keeping the baby—there is always outside professional help available in making your decision and in making it work.

Acknowledgments
Index

Acknowledgments

Many people helped to make this book possible. I wish to thank once again all the women who told me about their abortion experiences, those whose abortions I witnessed, and the hundreds whose anonymous abortion records I was able to study.

I would like to express my appreciation to all the hospital gynecologist-obstetricians, psychiatrists, nurses, and social workers who shared with me their time and experience. In particular I would like to thank the following, all of New York City: the Reverend William Brockman, of the American Foundation for Religion and Psychiatry; Dr. Lawrence Downs, clinical assistant professor of psychiatry, New York Hospital-Medical Center; the Reverend Jesse Lyons, of the Riverside

Church; Dr. Stanley Marinoff, director of the Division of Ambulatory Care of the Department of Obstetrics and Gynecology, Mount Sinai Hospital; Dr. Harold Marcus, associate clinical professor of psychiatry, Mount Sinai Hospital School of Medicine; Alfred F. Moran, executive vice president, Planned Parenthood of New York City; June Muyskens, of the National Clergy Consultation Service on Abortion; and Barbara Pyle, administrative director of Women's Services, an abortion clinic.

My very deepest gratitude goes to those who read various chapters of the book and who gave me valuable criticism and constructive suggestions: Ada Daniels, M.S.W., former director of the Family Planning Resources Center of Planned Parenthood of New York City; Dr. Marcel Heiman, clinical professor of psychiatry, Mount Sinai School of Medicine; Jimmye Kimmey, executive director, National Association for the Study of Abortion Laws; Dr. Bernard N. Nathanson, clinical professor of obstetrics and gynecology, Cornell University Medical College, associate attending in obstetrics and gynecology, New York Hospital-Cornell Medical Center, senior attending in obstetrics and gynecology, Women's Hospital, St. Luke's Hospital Center; and Linda Nessel, M.S.W., supervisor, Spence-Chapin Adoption Service.

Index

141

INDEX

142

psychological attitudes toward abortion, 40
psychological effects of abortion, 14–17

recovery, from abortion, 56
referral agencies, abortion, 49
repeated abortion, 89
reproductive capabilities, 63
residency requirements, 19
rhythm method, 110–111
Right to Abortion, The, 23
role of the father in unwanted pregnancy, 134

saline induction, 40, 57–58, 118
Second Sex, The, 38
self abortion attempts, 63
sexual mores, 21; relation to abortions, 83–85
speculum, 54
sperm banks, 114
spermicidal foam, 108–109
spontaneous abortion, 63
sterilization:
    female, 114–116
    male, 113–114
    reversal, 113–114
    surgical method, 115
Strong, Maurice, 22
suction curettage, 55; *see also* vacuum aspiration
Supreme Court, 13, 18–19, 25–27, 77

surgical methods of abortion, 51–69

therapeutic abortion, 79
tubal ligation, 114–115
Tufts Medical School, 120

underage girl:
    and abortion, 34
    and pregnancy, 127–132
United States Children's Bureau, 133
United States Supreme Court, 13, 18–19, 25–27, 77
unmarried woman, alternatives to abortion, 122–133
unwanted child, 24–25, 119, 123
uterine aspiration, 55, 60, 62, 118
uterine cancer, 99

vacuum aspiration, 55, 60, 62, 118
vaginal foaming tablets, 109
vasectomy, 113–114
venereal disease, 63

Washington, abortion ruling in, 18–19
welfare clients, and abortion, 21–22
withdrawal, 111
women's rights organizations, 23
World Health Organization, 21